Praise for Alice Miller and *The Body Never Lies*

"Alice Miller's arguments are lucid, closely reasoned, and utterly convincing." —Elaine Kendall, *Los Angeles Times Book Review*

"Alice Miller makes chillingly clear to the many what has been recognized only by the few: the extraordinary pain and psychological suffering inflicted on children under the guise of conventional childrearing."
—Maurice Sendak, author of *Where the Wild Things Are*

"In her brilliant book, Alice Miller uses famous people's lives, like Marcel Proust and Virginia Woolf, to teach us all a concept that is common in all of our lives—that unhealed trauma creates illness. I loved this book."
—Mona Lisa Schulz, author of *The New Feminine Brain* and *Awakening Intuition*

"As Alice Miller knows and makes so clear, the body remembers all the pain and suffering of childhood and exposes the abuses of childhood through physical symptoms in adolescence and adulthood, which she explores in this book. Readers will find much in this book that resonates with their own experiences and will learn how to confront the overt and covert traumas of their own childhoods with the enlightened guidance of Alice Miller."
—Philip Greven, professor emeritus, Rutgers University, and author of *Spare the Child: The Religious Roots of Punishment and the Psychological Impact of Physical Abuse*

"On her life journey of research and writing, Alice Miller has gained great inner freedom and strength. In *The Body Never Lies*, she courageously questions traditional morality and inspires us to face the often life-long pain that children suffer through their parents. Her profound insights into this vital relationship create a truthful vision of man and his coercion to be destructive and self-destructive."

—Barbara Rodgers, author of *Screams from Childhood*

"Few authors have championed the cause of the wounded child in all of us as Alice Miller has. In her latest masterpiece, *The Body Never Lies*, Miller's prose is, as ever, fearless and refreshingly direct. Miller breaks new ground as she tackles the most toxic cultural assumptions head-on, seeking to undo centuries of damage done to children by the most pervasive and most insidious of religious dogma. This book . . . points the way to healing and greater love through uncompromising emotional honesty. . . . [I]t is essential for counselors and psychotherapists who wish to cultivate their capacity for true empathy."

—Robin Grille, psychologist, author of
Parenting for a Peaceful World

"Alice Miller . . . follows her former distinguished works with a fascinating inquiry into the dire consequences for adults (physical illness, neurosis, psychosis) of their unacknowledged suffering as children at the hands of their parents. She takes the taboo subject out of the dark where Biblical dogma insists, "honor thy father and thy mother" and "spare the rod and spoil the child," and subjects it to the healing light of recognition and confronta-

tion. The sooner this examination of accepted child-rearing practice becomes common knowledge, the sooner we can repair it to
the benefit of children and the society they will create."
    —Jean Liedloff, author of *The Continuum Concept*

"Dr. Miller writes with astonishing and penetrating truth."
    —Norm Lee, author of *Of Moms and Moses*

Also by Alice Miller

The Drama of the Gifted Child:
The Search for the True Self
(originally published as *Prisoners of Childhood*)

For Your Own Good:
Hidden Cruelty in Child-rearing and the Roots of Violence

Thou Shalt Not Be Aware:
Society's Betrayal of the Child

Pictures of a Childhood:
Sixty-six Watercolors and an Essay

The Untouched Key:
Tracing Childhood Trauma in Creativity
and Destructiveness

Banished Knowledge:
Facing Childhood Injuries

Breaking Down the Wall of Silence:
The Liberating Experience of Facing Painful Truth

Paths of Life:
Seven Scenarios

The Truth Will Set You Free:
Overcoming Emotional Blindness

ALICE MILLER

The Body Never Lies

The Lingering Effects of Hurtful Parenting

Translated from the German by
Andrew Jenkins

W. W. Norton & Company
New York   London

Copyright © Suhrkamp Verlag Frankfurt am Main 2004
Copyright © for the English translation: Suhrkamp Verlag Frankfurt am Main 2005
Afterword copyright © 2006 by Alice Miller
Originally published in German as *Die Revolte des Körpers*

Manufacturing by LSC Harrisonburg
Book design by Chris Welch
Production manager: Amanda Morrison

Library of Congress Cataloging-in-Publication Data

Miller, Alice.
[Revolte des Körpers. English]
The body never lies : the lingering effects of cruel parenting / Alice Miller ;
translated from the German by Andrew Jenkins.
p. cm.
Includes bibliographical references.
ISBN 0-393-06065-9 (hardcover)
1. Child abuse—Psychological aspects. 2. Family violence—Psychological aspects.
3. Discipline of children—Psychological aspects. 4. Parenting—Psychological aspects.
5. Adult child abuse victims—Mental health. 6. Abused children—Mental health.
7. Authors—Psychology. 8. Medicine, Psychosomatic. 9. Parent and child. 10. Cruelty.
I. Title.
RC569.5.C55M55713 2004
616.85'82239—dc22
2005004299

ISBN 978-0-393-32863-9 pbk.

W. W. Norton & Company, Inc., 500 Fifth Avenue, New York, N.Y. 10110
www.wwnorton.com

W. W. Norton & Company Ltd., 15 Carlisle Street, London W1D 3BS

Emotions are not a luxury,
they are a complex aid
in the fight for existence.

— ANTONIO R. DAMASIO

Contents

II

TRADITIONAL MORALITY IN THERAPY AND THE KNOWLEDGE OF THE BODY

III

ANOREXIA: THE LONGING FOR GENUINE COMMUNICATION

Preface

THE CENTRAL ISSUE in all my books is the denial of
the sufferings we have undergone in childhood. Each of
these books revolves around a particular aspect of this
phenomenon and emphasizes one theme more strongly than
another. In *For Your Own Good* and *Thou Shalt Not Be Aware*, for
example, I concentrate on the causes and consequences of this
denial. In later works I have explored its impact on the lives of
adults and on society (with special reference to art and philosophy in *The Untouched Key*, and to politics and psychiatry in
Breaking Down the Wall of Silence). As these different aspects
cannot be examined in complete isolation, there is invariably a
small degree of overlap and repetition. But the attentive reader
will readily appreciate that recurring topics appear in a different
light depending on the context in which they are addressed and
the vantage point from which they are viewed.

One thing that has nothing to do with context, however, is the way in which I employ certain concepts. For example, I use the word "unconscious" exclusively to refer to repressed, denied, or disassociated content (memories, emotions, needs). For me, a person's unconscious is nothing other than his/her biography, a life story that, although stored in the body in its entirety, is accessible to our consciousness only in a highly fragmentary form. Accordingly, I never use the word "truth" in a metaphysical sense. The meaning I give it is invariably that of a subjective entity, related to the actual life of the individual concerned. This is why I frequently speak of "his" or "her" truth, meaning the true story of the person in question, as evidenced by and reflected in his/her emotions (see p. 38 and pp. 125 and 174). In my terminology, emotion is a more or less unconscious, but at the same time vitally important physical response to internal or external events—such things as fear of thunderstorms, rage at having been deceived, or the pleasure that results from a present we really desire. By contrast, the word "feeling" designates a *conscious* perception of an emotion. Emotional blindness, then, is usually a (self-)destructive luxury that we indulge in at our cost.

MY MAIN CONCERN in this present book is with the effects the denial of our true and strong emotions have on our bodies. Such denial is demanded of us not least by morality and religion. On the basis of what I know about psychotherapy, both from personal experience and from accounts I have been given by very many people, I have come to the conclusion that individuals abused in childhood can attempt to obey the Fourth Commandment* only by recourse to a massive repression and detachment

---

* "Honor thy father and thy mother," as in the Roman Catholic and Lutheran

of their true emotions. They cannot love and honor their parents because unconsciously they still fear them. However much they may want to, they cannot build up a relaxed and trusting relationship.

Instead, what usually materializes is a pathological attachment, a mixture of fear and dutiful obedience that hardly deserves the name of love in the genuine sense of the word. I call this a sham, a façade. In addition, people abused in childhood frequently hope all their lives that someday they will experience the love they have been denied. These expectations reinforce their attachment to their parents, an attachment that religious creeds refer to as love and praise as a virtue. Unfortunately, the same thing happens in most therapies, as most people are still dominated by traditional morality. There is a price to be paid for this morality, a price paid by the body.

Individuals who believe that they feel what they ought to feel and constantly do their best not to feel what they forbid themselves to feel will ultimately fall ill—unless, that is, they leave it to their children to pick up the check by projecting onto them the emotions they cannot admit to themselves.

This book reveals a psychobiological law that has been concealed for a very long time by the claims of religion and morality.

Its first part demonstrates how this law affected the lives and careers of a number of writers and other famous personalities. Subsequent sections provide ways for achieving genuine communication, which can break the vicious circle of self-deception and often lead to liberation from physical symptoms.

---

tradition. In the Eastern Orthodox faith and in most Protestant denominations, as well as in the Jewish tradition, this is numbered as the Fifth Commandment.

The Body
Never Lies

.

Introduction

Morality and the Body

F REQUENTLY, PHYSICAL ILLNESSES are the body's response to permanent disregard of its vital functions. One of our most vital functions is an ability to listen to the true story of our own lives. Accordingly, the central issue in this book is the conflict between the things we feel—the things our bodies register—and the things we think we *ought* to feel so as to comply with moral norms and standards we have internalized at a very early age. It is my firm and considered opinion that one specific and extremely well-established behavior norm—the Fourth Commandment—frequently prevents us from admitting to our true feelings, and that we pay for this compromise with various forms of physical illness. *The Body Never Lies* contains many examples that substantiate this theory. My focus, however, is not on entire biographies, but rather on the relationship between individuals and the parents who were responsible for the kind of cruelty and abuse outlined.

Experience has taught me that my own body is the source of all the vital information that has enabled me to achieve greater autonomy and self-confidence. Only when I allowed myself to feel the emotions pent up for so long inside me did I start extricating myself from my own past. Genuine feelings are never the product of conscious effort. They are quite simply there, and they are there for a very good reason, even if that reason is not always apparent. I cannot force myself to love or honor my parents if my body rebels against such an endeavor for reasons that are well-known to it. But if I still attempt to obey the Fourth Commandment, then the upshot will be the kind of stress that is invariably involved when I demand the impossible of myself. This kind of stress has accompanied me almost all my life. Anxious to stay in line with the system of moral values I had accepted, I did my best to imagine good feelings I did not possess while ignoring the bad feelings I did have. My aim was to be loved as a daughter. But the effort was all in vain. In the end I had to realize that I cannot force love to come if it is not there in the first place. On the other hand, I learned that a feeling of love will establish itself automatically (for example, love for my children or love for my friends) once I stop demanding that I feel such love and stop obeying the moral injunctions imposed on me. But such a sensation can happen only when I feel free and remain open and receptive to all my feelings, including the negative ones.

The realization that I cannot manipulate my feelings, that I can delude neither myself nor others, brought me immense relief and liberation. Only then was I fully struck by the large number of people who (like myself) literally almost kill themselves in the attempt to obey the Fourth Commandment, without any consideration of the price this exacts both from their own bodies and from their children. As long as the children allow themselves to be used in this way, it is entirely possible to live to be one hundred without any awareness of one's own personal truth and without any illness ensuing from this protracted form of self-deception.

A mother who is forced to realize that the deprivations imposed on her in her youth make it impossible for her to love a child of her own, however hard she may try, can certainly expect to be accused of immorality if she has the courage to put that truth into words. But I believe that it is precisely this explicit acceptance of her true feelings, independent of the claims of morality, that will enable her to give both herself and her children the honest and sincere kind of support they need most, and at the same time will allow her to free herself from the shackles of self-deception.

When children are born, what they need most from their parents is love, by which I mean affection, attention, care, protection, kindness, and the willingness to communicate. If these needs are gratified, the bodies of those children will retain the good memory of such caring affection all their lives, and later, as adults, they will be able to pass on the same kind of love to their children. But if this is not the case, the children will be left with a lifelong yearning for the fulfillment of their initial (and vital) needs. In later life, this yearning will be directed at other people. In comparison, the more implacably children have been deprived of love and negated or maltreated in the name of "upbringing," the more those children, on reaching adulthood, will look to their parents (or other people substituting for them) to supply all the things that those same parents failed to provide when they were needed most. This is a normal response on the part of the body. It knows precisely what it needs, it cannot forget the deprivations. The deprivation or hole is there, waiting to be filled.

The older we get, the more difficult it is to find other people who can give us the love our parents denied us. But the body's expectations do not slacken with age—quite the contrary! They are merely directed at others, usually our own children and grandchildren. The only way out of this dilemma is to become aware of these mechanisms and to identify the reality of our own childhood by counteracting the processes of repression and denial. In this way we can create in our own selves a person who can satisfy at least some of the needs that have been waiting for fulfillment since birth, if not earlier. Then we can give ourselves the attention, the respect, the understanding for our emotions, the sorely needed protection, and the unconditional love that our parents withheld from us.

To make this happen, we need one special experience: the experience of love for the child we once were. Without it, we have no way of knowing what love consists of. If we want to achieve this experience with the help of therapy, then we need assistance from a therapist who can accept us for what we are, who can give us the protection, respect, sympathy, and understanding we need in order to realize how we have become what we are. This is the fundamental experience that enables us to adopt the role of parents for the wronged children we once were. What we do *not* need is an educator, someone who "has plans" for us, nor a psychoanalyst who has learned that in the face of childhood traumas the main thing is to remain neutral and interpret the analysand's reports as fantasies. No, we need precisely the opposite: a *partial* companion, someone who can share with us the horror and indignation that is bound to arise when our emotions gradually reveal to her, and to us, how the little child suffered, what it went through all alone when body and soul were fighting for years on end to preserve a life threatened by constant danger. We need such a companion—what I have called an "enlightened witness"—if we ourselves are to act as companions for the child within, if we are to understand its "body language," to engage with its needs instead of ignoring them in the same way that our parents once did.

What I am describing here is entirely realistic. It is possible to find out one's own truth in the partial, *non-neutral* company of such a (therapeutic) companion. In that process one can shed one's symptoms, free oneself of depression, regain joy in life, break out of the state of constant exhaustion, and experience a resurgence of energy, once that energy is no longer required for the repression of one's own truth. The point is that the fatigue characteristic of such depression reasserts itself every time we repress strong emotions, play down the memories stored in the body, and refuse them the attention they clamor for.

Why are such positive developments the exception rather than the rule? Why do most people (including the "experts") greatly prefer to believe in the power of medication rather than let themselves be guided by the knowledge stored in their own bodies? Our bodies know exactly what we need, what we have been denied, what disagrees with us, what we are allergic to. But many people prefer to seek aid from medication, drugs, or alcohol, which can only block off the path to the understanding of the truth even more completely. Why? Because recognizing the truth is painful? This is certainly the case. But that pain is temporary. With the right kind of therapeutic care it can be endured. I believe that the main problem here is that there are not enough such professional companions to be had. Almost all the representatives of what I'll call the "caring professions" appear to be prevented by our morality system from siding with the children we once were and recognizing the consequences of the early injuries we have sustained. They are entirely under the influence of the Fourth Commandment, which tells us to honor our parents, "that thy days may be long upon the land the Lord thy God giveth thee."

It is patently obvious that this commandment is bound to thwart the healing of early injuries. It is equally obvious why this fact has never been publicly recognized and thought about. The scope and power of the commandment is immeasurable, since it is nurtured by the infant's natural attachment to its parents. The greatest philosophers and writers have shied away from attacking it. Even Friedrich Nietzsche, who was notable for his virulent attacks on Christian morality, never went so far as to extend that criticism to his own family. In every adult who has suffered abuse as a child lies dormant that small child's fear of punishment at the hands of the parents if he or she should dare to rebel against their behavior. But it will lie dormant only as long as that fear remains unconscious. Once consciously experienced, it will dissolve in the course of time.

The morality behind the Fourth Commandment, coupled with the expectations of the children we once were, creates a situation in which the large majority of therapists will offer patients precisely the same principles they were confronted with during their upbringing. Many of these therapists are still bound up with their own parents by countless threads. They call this inextricable entanglement "love," and offer this kind of love to others as a solution. They preach forgiveness as a path to recovery and appear not to know that this path is a trap by which they themselves are caught. Forgiveness has never had a healing effect.[1]

It is highly significant, perplexing to say the least, that we have been bound for thousands of years to a commandment that hardly anyone has questioned, simply because it underscores the physical reality that all children, whether abused or not, always love their parents. Only as adults do we have a choice. But we often behave as if we were still children who never had the right to question the commandments laid down to them by their parents. As conscious adults we have the right to pose questions, even though we know how much those questions would have shocked our parents when we were children.

Moses, who imposed the Ten Commandments on his people in the name of God, was himself a child cast out by his parents. The situation that prompted them to do so is immaterial. Like most abandoned children, he hoped that one day he might regain his parents' love by providing them with such things as understanding and respect. We are told that he was forsaken by his parents to save him from persecution. But the infant in the basket of bulrushes could hardly have understood that. The adult Moses may indeed have said, "My parents cast me adrift in order to protect me. I cannot hold that against them. They deserve my gratitude. They saved my life." But what Moses the child actually felt might have been something very different: "Why have my parents cast me out? Why have they exposed me to the danger of drowning? Don't they love me?" The authentic feelings stored up in the body of the little infant—despair and mortal fear—will have lived on in Moses and dictated his actions when he passed the Ten Commandments on to his people. Superficially, the Fourth Commandment can be regarded as a kind of life insurance for old people, which was perhaps necessary in biblical times but is certainly no longer required in this form. On closer inspection, however, we see that the Fourth Commandment contains a threat, a kind of moral blackmail that has lost none of its potency: If you want to live a long life, you have to honor your parents, even if they do not deserve it; otherwise you will die an early death.

Most people comply with this injunction, although it is both confusing and frightening. My belief is that the time has come for us to take the injuries of childhood and their consequences seriously. We must free ourselves of this commandment. This does not mean that we have to repay our parents' cruelty in kind. It means that we must see them as they were, and recognize the way they treated us when we were small. Then we can spare ourselves and our children the repetition of such patterns of behavior. We need to free ourselves of the "internalized parents" carrying on their deadly work within us. This is the only way we can say yes to our own lives and learn to respect ourselves. It is not something we can learn from Moses. Moses became disloyal to the messages of his own body when he espoused the Fourth Commandment. He had no choice in the matter for he was not aware of these messages. But this is precisely the reason for not allowing this commandment to assert its power over us.

In all my books I have attempted to demonstrate, in different ways and in different contexts, how the effects of what I've called "poisonous pedagogy" that we experienced as children have stunted our vitality in later life and also substantially impaired, if not entirely killed off, the feeling for who we really are, what we feel, and what we need. The parenting approach known as "poisonous pedagogy" breeds overly well-adjusted individuals who can only trust the mask they have been forced to wear because as children they lived in constant fear of punishment. "I am bringing you up in the way that is best for you" is the supreme principle behind this approach. "If I beat you or use words to torment and humiliate you, it is all for your own good."[2]

In his famous novel *Fateless*, the Hungarian writer and Nobel laureate Imre Kertész describes his arrival at the Auschwitz concentration camp. He was fifteen years old at the time, and he tells us in great detail how he attempted to interpret the many grotesque and appalling things he encountered on his arrival there as something positive and favorable for him. Otherwise he would not have survived his own mortal fear.

Probably every child who has suffered abuse must assume an attitude like this in order to survive. These children reinterpret their perceptions in a desperate attempt to see as good and beneficial things that outside observers would immediately classify as crimes. Children have no choice. They must repress their true feelings if they have no "helping witness" to turn to and are helplessly exposed to their persecutors. Later, as adults lucky enough to encounter "enlightened witnesses," they do have a choice. Then they can admit the truth, *their* truth; they can stop pitying and "understanding" their persecutors, stop trying to feel their unsustainable, disassociated emotions, and roundly denounce the things that have been done to them. This step brings immense relief for the body. It no longer has to forcibly remind the adult self of the tragic history it went through as a child. Once the adult self has decided to find out the whole truth about itself, the body feels understood, respected, and protected.

I call the violent kind of "upbringing" abuse, not only because children are thus refused the right to dignity and respect as human beings but also because such an approach to parenting establishes a kind of totalitarian regime in which it is impossible for children to perceive the humiliations, indignities, and disrespect they have been subjected to, let alone to defend themselves against them. These patterns of childhood will inevitably then be adopted by their victims and used on their partners and their own children, at work, in politics, wherever the fear and anxiety of the profoundly insecure child can be fended off with the aid of external power. It is in this way that dictators are born; these are people with a deep-seated contempt for everyone else, people who were never respected as children and thus do their utmost to earn that respect at a later stage with the assistance of the gigantic power apparatus they have built up around them.

The sphere of politics is an excellent example of the way in which the hunger for power and recognition is never stilled. It is insatiable, it can never be entirely satisfied. The more power these people have, the more they are spurred on to actions that, in a process of compulsory repetition, restore the initial feelings of impotence they were trying to escape: Hitler in his bunker, Stalin in his paranoid fears, Mao in the final rejection by his people, Napoleon in exile, Milosevic in prison, Saddam Hussein in his mortifying fall from power. What impelled these men to abuse the power they had achieved to such a pitch that it ultimately plunged them into impotence and powerlessness? I believe it was their bodies. Their bodies sustained the knowledge of the impotence they felt in childhood; they stored such knowledge in their cells, and they set out to force their "owners" to face up to that knowledge. But the reality of their childhood instilled such fear in the hearts of these dictators that they preferred to wipe out whole peoples, to exterminate millions of human beings, rather than confront the truth—*their* truth.

In this book I shall not be enlarging on the motives of such dictators, although I find the study of their biographies highly illuminating. I shall concentrate instead on people, who, though they too were subjected to poisonous pedagogy, did not feel the need to achieve limitless power or to become dictators. In contrast to those power-crazed individuals, they did not direct the suppressed feelings of anger and indignation against others, but against themselves. They fell ill and developed a variety of symptoms, and many of them died at an early age.

The more gifted of these individuals became writers or artists. Even though they were able to point to the truth in the literature and art they produced, it was invariably a truth split off from their own lives. The price for that maneuver was illness. The first part of the book is devoted to tragic biographies of this kind.

A RESEARCH TEAM in San Diego in the 1990s asked a total of 17,000 people, with an average age of fifty-seven, what their childhood was like and what illnesses they had suffered in the course of their lives. The study revealed that the incidence of severe illnesses was many times higher in people who had been abused in their childhood than in people who had grown up free of such abuse and had never been exposed to beatings meted out to them "for their own good." The latter had had no illnesses to speak of in their later lives. The title of this brief article was "Turning Gold into Lead." [3] The author, who sent me this article, commented that these findings are unambiguous and highly eloquent, but at the same time covert and hidden.

Why hidden? The reason is that they cannot be published without leveling accusations at the parents. And that is something that is still prohibited in our society, in fact to an increasing degree. In the meantime, more and more experts are of the opinion that the psychic sufferings of adults can be traced to genetic heredity, rather than to concrete injuries and parental deprivations in childhood. Also, the enlightening studies on the childhood of schizophrenics that were published in medical journals in the 1970s have never been made known to a wider public. The fundamentalist faith in genetics continues to triumph.

This state of affairs is the subject of the book *They F*** You Up* by Oliver James, a clinical psychologist with a major reputation in the United Kingdom. Although the impression left by the book, published in 2003, is ambivalent (because the author shies away from the consequences of his insights and expressly warns against assigning parents the responsibility for the sufferings of their children), this study draws upon numerous research results to prove beyond doubt that genetic factors, in fact, play a very minor role in the development of psychic disorders.

Accordingly, many present-day therapies are careful to avoid the subject of childhood.[4] True, patients are initially encouraged to admit to the strong emotions they have. But when emotions are aroused in this way they are normally accompanied by repressed memories of childhood, memories of abuse, exploitation, humiliation, and hurt suffered in the first few years of life. This is something a therapist can deal with only if he has explored those avenues himself. Therapists of this kind are still rare. So what most of them offer their clients is a rehash of poisonous pedagogy, precisely the same brand of morality that made them ill in the first place.

The body cannot understand this kind of morality; it will have no truck with the Fourth Commandment, and it cannot be fooled by words in the way the mind can. The body is the guardian of the truth, *our* truth, because it carries the experience of a lifetime and ensures that we can live with the truth of our organism. With the aid of physical symptoms it forces us to engage cognitively with this truth so that we can communicate harmoniously with the child within, the child who lives on inside us, the child who was once spurned, abused, and humiliated.

I MYSELF EXPERIENCED physical "correction" in the first few months of my life. Of course I lived for decades in total ignorance of this fact. My mother told me that I was such a good girl that she never had any trouble with me. She also attributed my "goodness" to the consistent application of her upbringing methods from earliest infancy. This also explains why I had absolutely no memories of that period for such a long time. They started coming back only as a result of the strong emotions uncovered by the last course of therapy I underwent. While those emotions initially expressed themselves in connection with persons other than my parents, I gradually managed to locate their true origins, to integrate them as understandable feelings and thus to reconstruct the history of my early childhood. In this way I lost my old, hitherto incomprehensible fears and was able, thanks to the partial companionship of my therapist, finally to let new tissue grow over the old wounds.

Those fears were bound up primarily with my need for communication, a need that my mother not only did not respond to, but also, consistent with her stringent upbringing methods, actively punished as if it were something reprehensible. The quest for contact and exchange expressed itself initially in the form of crying, then in a desire to ask questions, and finally in the communication of my own thoughts and feelings. But my crying was punished with slaps, my questions were answered with lies, and the expression of my thoughts and feelings was quite simply forbidden. My mother's withdrawal into a silence that sometimes lasted for days was a constantly impending threat. As she never wanted me to be the way I really was, I had to actively conceal my authentic feelings from her.

My mother was prone to fits of towering rage, but she was completely incapable of reflection and never sought to investigate the reasons for her emotions. Because, ever since childhood, she had lived a life marred by frustration and dissatisfaction, she was constantly accusing me of something or other. Whenever I defended myself against this unjust treatment, sometimes going so far as to actually prove my innocence to her, she interpreted this as a systematic attack on her person and frequently retaliated with ferocious punishments. She confused emotions with facts. As she *felt* attacked by my explanations, she took it for granted that I was actually attacking her. A capacity for reflection would have been necessary for her to realize that the real reasons for her feelings had nothing to do with my behavior. But remorse was completely foreign to her. Not once did she apologize to me or express any kind of regret. She was always "in the right." It was this attitude that made my childhood feel like a totalitarian regime.

IN THIS BOOK I expound my theory about the destructive power of the Fourth Commandment in three different sections. Part I contains vignettes taken from the lives of different writers who, though they unconsciously revealed the truth about their childhood in their works, were never able to admit this truth to their conscious minds because of the infant fear that lived on in them in a disassociated state. Even in adulthood, the child within could not believe that he/she would not be killed if the truth were told. Because this fear is supported, not only in our society but all over the world, by a commandment that admonishes us to be lenient and forgiving to our parents, it has remained disassociated and thus impervious to any attempts to come to terms with it. The price we pay for this so-called solution, for an evasion that results in the idealization of our parents, for denial of the real dangers we were exposed to in our early lives and the justified fears those dangers leave behind in our bodies, is very high, as we shall see in the examples of the writers whose stories I'll examine. Unfortunately, I could add countless others. The unambiguous message communicated by these examples is that the individuals involved paid for the attachment to their parents with severe illness, premature death, or suicide. The attempt to conceal the truth about the sufferings they went through in early childhood stood in crass contradiction to the knowledge stored in their bodies. Their writing helped them to express that knowledge but did nothing to make them consciously aware of it. Accordingly, their bodies—the spurned and humiliated children within—still did not feel understood and respected. The central point in all this is that the body cannot relate to the commandments of morality. Ethical concerns are entirely alien to it. Bodily functions like breathing, circulation, digestion respond only to *the emotions we actually feel*, not to moral precepts. The body sticks to the facts.

Ever since I began thinking about the influence of childhood on our later lives, I have spent a lot of time reading the diaries and letters of writers I am particularly interested in. What I found there has given me many a key to a closer understanding of their works, their central concerns, and also their sufferings. Although these sufferings are traceable to their childhood experiences, their tragic nature remained inaccessible to the conscious minds and the emotional lives of these writers. Even though the personal tragedies of writers like Dostoevsky, Nietzsche, and Rimbaud are apparent in their works, their various biographies don't mention them. These books contained an abundance of detail on the lives of the respective authors and a plethora of factual information but there was hardly any indication of how they attempted to come to terms with their childhood traumas, the effects these traumas had on them, and the way they marked the course of their lives. When I approached literary scholars for enlightenment on this point, I found that they had little or no interest in the subject. Most of them reacted to my inquiries with embarrassment, as if I had confronted them with something indecent, almost obscene. Their response was evasive in the extreme.

But there were exceptions. One or two of these scholars showed an interest in the approach I proposed and came up with precious biographical material that they had long been familiar with but that had hitherto appeared insignificant to them. It is this material, overlooked or ignored by most biographers, that I have concentrated on in the first part of this book. Inevitably, this has involved restricting myself to one particular aspect of these authors' lives, leaving aside other facets that are perhaps of equal importance. While this may provoke criticism of one-sidedness or reductionism, I have elected to pursue this course because I do not want an abundance of detail to divert the reader's attention from the unifying thread that runs through this book—the focus on morality and the body.

All the writers referred to here, with the possible exception of Kafka, were not aware that as children they had suffered immensely at the hands of their parents. Accordingly, they "bore them no grudges" in later life, at least not consciously. It would be entirely unrealistic to assume that they could have confronted their parents with the truth, for it was a truth that those adult children were ignorant of. Their conscious minds had repressed it.

This unawareness is indeed the tragedy that in most cases shortened their lives. *Morality prevented them from recognizing reality,* the truth enshrined in the bodies of these highly gifted individuals. They could not see that they were sacrificing their lives to their parents, even when, like Schiller, they fought for the cause of liberty, or, like Rimbaud and Mishima, broke with all moral taboos (on the face of it), or, like Joyce, upended the literary and aesthetic canons of the day, or, like Proust, trained a merciless gaze on the bourgeoisie (while at the same time averting that gaze from their own sufferings at the hands of their bourgeois parents). I have concentrated on these aspects because, as far as I know, there have been no publications on them from the perspective I have adopted here.

IN *THE BODY NEVER LIES*, I take up a number of thoughts from my earlier works in order to cast light on them from this new perspective and also to investigate various questions that have so far remained unanswered. Since Wilhelm Reich and Arthur Janov, therapeutic experience has repeatedly shown that strong emotions are indeed retrievable. But only now do we have well-substantiated explanations for this phenomenon, as a result of the work of brain researchers like Joseph LeDoux, Antonio R. Damasio, Bruce D. Perry, and numerous others. On the one hand, we know today that our bodies keep a complete and fault-less record of all the things we have ever experienced. On the other, we know that, thanks to therapeutic engagement with our emotions, we are no longer doomed to passing them on blindly to our children or living them out at our own expense. Accordingly, in Part II, I report on individuals who are prepared unflinchingly to confront the truth about their childhood and to see their parents in a realistic light. Unfortunately, it is very often the case that therapeutic success can be seriously endangered if therapy (as frequently happens) is subjected to the dictates of conventional morality, thus making it impossible for adult clients to free themselves of the compulsive persuasion that they owe their parents love and gratitude. The authentic feelings stored in the body remain untapped, and the price the clients have to pay for this is the unremitting persistence of the severe symptoms affecting them. I assume that readers who have themselves undergone a number of unsuccessful therapies will readily recognize their plight in this problem.

In my investigations of the connections between morality and the body, I encountered two further aspects that, unlike the problem of forgiveness, were new to me. One question I asked myself concerned the true nature of the feeling that we, as adults, persist in calling love for our parents. The other aspect that struck me was the realization that throughout our lives the body craves the nourishment that it needed so badly in child-hood but was never given. I believe that this is a source of suf-fering and distress for many people.

Part III examines a particularly "telling" disorder to show how the body defends itself against the wrong kind of nourishment. What it needs above all else is the truth. As long as this truth remains unidentified and a person's genuine feelings about his/her parents continue to be ignored, the body has no choice but to go on producing symptoms. My intention in this part of the book is to use simple, everyday language to point to the tragedy of patients with eating disorders who have grown up without any genuine emotional exchange with others and who are denied this kind of exchange in later therapy. I sincerely hope that this description will help some patients with eating disorders to achieve a better understanding of their condition. In addition, "The Fictional Diary of Anita Fink" points a finger at a source of despair that is by no means restricted to anorexics: the failure to achieve genuine communication with the parents in childhood, despite all the fruitless attempts undertaken to bring this about. But in adulthood, once there are prospects for authentic exchanges with other people, this futile quest can gradually be relinquished.

THE TRADITION OF sacrificing children is deeply rooted in most cultures and religions. For this reason it is also tolerated, and indeed commended, in our western civilization. Naturally, we no longer sacrifice our sons and daughters on the altar of God, as in the biblical story of Abraham and Isaac. But at birth and throughout their later upbringing, we instill in them the necessity to love, honor, and respect us, to do their best for us, to satisfy our ambitions—in short, to give us everything our parents denied us. We call this decency and morality. Children rarely have any choice in the matter. All their lives, they will force themselves to offer their parents something that they neither possess nor have any knowledge of, quite simply because they have never been given it: genuine, unconditional love that does not merely serve to gratify the needs of the recipient. Yet they will continue to strive in this direction because even as adults they still believe that they need their parents and because, despite all the disappointments they have experienced, they still hope for some token of genuine affection from those parents.

Such futile striving can have fateful effects on adult children if they are unable to free themselves of this urge. All it results in is delusion, compulsion, pretense, and self-deception.

The strong desire of many parents to be loved and honored by their children finds great legitimization in the Fourth Commandment. In a television broadcast I once happened to watch, the representatives of various religions asserted that we must honor our parents, regardless of what they have done to us. In this way, the dependency of children on their parents is reinforced, and those who believe in this tenet are kept ignorant of the fact that, as adults, it is entirely possible for them to liberate themselves from this cycle. In the light of present-day knowledge, we see that the Fourth Commandment is in fact a contradiction in terms. A system of morality tells us what to do and what not to do, but it cannot tell us what we should feel. Genuine feelings cannot be produced, nor can they be eradicated. We can only repress them, delude ourselves, and deceive our bodies. But as we have already seen, our brains are permanent repositories of our emotions; these are retrievable, susceptible of experience, and luckily they can be transformed without risk into conscious feelings. And if we are fortunate enough to find an enlightened witness, we can learn to recognize their meaning and their causes.

The strange idea of having to love God so that He does not punish me for my rebelliousness and disappointment, but instead rewards me with the love that forgives all, becomes just as much the expression of our childish dependency and insecurity as the assumption that, like our parents, God is in desperate need of our love. But is this not a completely grotesque idea? A higher being dependent on inauthentic feelings dictated by morality is strongly reminiscent of the insecurity displayed by our frustrated and disoriented parents. Such a being can be called God only by people who have never questioned their own parents or thought about their dependency on them.

The Painter

I

⌇⌇⌇

SAYING
AND
CONCEALING

For I would prefer to have these attacks
and please you, rather than displease you
and not have them.

—*Marcel Proust in a letter to his mother*

1

Awe of the Parents and
Its Tragic Effects

Dostoevsky, Chekhov, Kafka, Nietzsche

THE WORKS OF the Russian writers Dostoevsky and Chekhov meant a great deal to me in my youth. My later studies of these authors have shown me how faultlessly the disassociative mechanism functions, not only today but also over a century ago. When I finally succeeded in giving up the illusions I had entertained about my parents and recognized the effects of their deeds on my life as a whole, this also opened my eyes to facts I had formerly not attributed any importance to. Janko Lavrin's biography of Dostoevsky informed me that in later life his father, initially an army doctor, inherited an estate with more than a hundred serfs. His treatment of these people was so brutal that they eventually summoned up the courage to murder him. The conclusion I drew from this was that his brutality must have far exceeded the norm, for what other explanation could there be for the fact that these cowed vassals elected to run the risk of banishment for their crime, rather than suffering any longer under this reign of terror? It thus seemed more than plausible that his eldest son would also have been subjected to some kind of cruelty. Accordingly, I resolved to investigate how the author of so many world-famous novels had managed to come to terms with his own personal history. I was of course familiar with his portrayal of a merciless father in *The Brothers Karamazov*, but I wanted to find out what his relationship with his real father was like. First I looked for relevant passages in his letters. I read them all but found not one single instance of a letter to his father. The one and only mention of him was obviously designed to testify to the son's consummate respect and unconditional love for him. On the other hand, almost all his letters to other people contained complaints about his financial situation and requests for financial support. To my mind, all these letters clearly express a child's fear of the constant threat to his very existence, coupled with the desperate hope that the addressee will understand his distress and be kindly disposed to him.

It is a well-known fact that Dostoevsky's health was extremely poor. He suffered from chronic insomnia and complained of dreadful nightmares, in which we may assume that his childhood traumas found a way of expressing themselves without his becoming consciously aware of the fact. We also know that for decades Dostoevsky suffered epileptic fits. But his biographers make little or no indication of any connection between these attacks and his traumatic childhood. They have been equally blind to the yearning for a merciful destiny that is clearly recognizable in his addiction to roulette. Though his wife helped him to overcome this addiction, she was unable to function as an enlightened witness because at the time it was thought to be even more reprehensible to level accusations at one's own father than it is now.

I HAVE IDENTIFIED a similar struggle in the life of Anton Chekhov. In his short story "The Father," he gives what I think is probably an extremely accurate account of the character of his own father, a former serf and an alcoholic. The man in the story is an inveterate drinker who lives off his sons and basks in the reflected glory of their successes, thus attempting to suppress his own sense of futility. He makes no effort to see who his sons really are and never displays any feelings of affection or human dignity.

This story is classified as fiction, and probably its biographical significance was completely split off from Anton's conscious life. If the author had been able to see and feel how his father had actually treated him, he would undoubtedly have been plunged into profound shame or goaded into righteous anger. But at the time such a reaction was unthinkable. Instead of rebelling against his father, Chekhov supported the whole family, even in the earlier stages of his career when he was earning very little. He paid for his parents' apartment in Moscow and devotedly looked after them and his brothers. But in his correspondence I found very little mention of his father. Such passages as there are testify to the entirely benevolent and understanding attitude adopted by the son. There are no traces of indignation at the cruel blows he received almost daily from his father in his youth. In his early thirties, Chekhov spent some months on the island of Sakhalin, a penal colony. His intention, so he said, was to describe the lives of the condemned, the tormented, and the tortured. The knowledge that he was in fact one of their number

was presumably split off from his own awareness. His biographers attribute his early death at the age of forty-four, to the
appalling conditions and extreme cold that prevailed on the
island. But we should not forget that, like his brother Nikolai,
who was killed by the illness at an even younger age, Chekhov
suffered from tuberculosis almost all his life.

IN *THOU SHALT NOT BE AWARE*, in reference to the life
of Franz Kafka and other writers, I said that, while writing helped
them to survive, it was not enough to liberate the child imprisoned within, nor to restore the vitality, sensitivity, and security
that child had forfeited. For this process of liberation an enlightened witness is indispensable.

There were witnesses to Kafka's sufferings, both his great love
Milena Jesenská and, above all, his sister Ottla. He was able to
confide in them about most things but not about his early anxieties and the way he suffered at the hands of his parents. Those
remained taboo. Ultimately, he actually did go so far as to write
the famous *Letter to His Father.* However, he sent it not to his
father but to his mother, requesting that she pass it on to the
addressee. In her he sought the enlightened witness, hoping that
after reading the letter she would finally understand his sufferings and offer to act as a mediator between himself and his
father. But his mother held the letter back and never made any
attempt to talk to her son about what it contained. And without
the support of an enlightened witness, Kafka was unable to confront his father himself. The threat of punishment was far too
menacing. We need only recall the stories *The Judgment* or *The
Metamorphosis* to appreciate how far his fears of such a threat
actually went. Unfortunately, Kafka had no one who might have

encouraged him to overcome these fears and send off the letter. If he had, it might have saved his life. He was unable to undertake this step alone, contracted tuberculosis, and died in his early forties.

I HAVE ALSO observed similar parallels in the life of Friedrich Nietzsche, whose tragedy I have described in *The Untouched Key* and *Breaking Down the Wall of Silence*. I interpret Nietzsche's magnificent achievement as a protracted cry for liberation from lies, exploitation, hypocrisy, and his own overadjustment. No one—least of all Nietzsche himself—could see how he had suffered from all this as a small child. But his body labored unremittingly under this burden. The young Nietzsche suffered from rheumatism, a condition that, like his severe headaches, can certainly be attributed to the retention of strong emotions. He was also affected by countless other complaints, as many as one hundred in the course of a single year at school. No one could have realized that the actual source of his suffering was the mendacious morality that governed his everyday life. All those around him breathed the same air as he did. But his body absorbed this hypocrisy far more acutely than others. If someone had helped Nietzsche to admit the knowledge stored in his body, he might not have had to "lose his mind" in order to remain blind to his own truth for the rest of his life.

2

The Fight for Liberty in the Dramas and the Unheeded Outcry of the Body

Friedrich von Schiller

E VEN TODAY, we frequently hear the view expressed that no lasting harm is done to children who get slapped or spanked from time to time. Many people believe their own lives are the best proof of this conviction. But they can uphold such a belief only as long as the connections between the illnesses they have suffered in adulthood and the blows they received in childhood remain concealed. The example of Friedrich von Schiller underscores how powerfully such concealment can function. In the course of the centuries, its effects have been accepted uncritically and passed on from one generation to the next.

Friedrich von Schiller, one of the greatest Romantic playwrights and writers of the eighteenth century, spent the all-important first three years of his life in the sole company of his loving mother. Under her care he was able to develop his character and his enormous talents to the full. Only when he was four did his despotic father return from the wars. Biographer Friedrich Burschell describes him as a strict, impatient, choleric man "with a species of stubborn and restricted egotism." Essentially, his idea of upbringing was to suppress all the manifestations of spontaneity and creativity displayed by his lively little son. Despite this, Schiller was an achiever at school, due largely to his intelligence and the self-assurance he had been able to cultivate in the atmosphere of emotional security provided by his mother in the first three years of his life. At the age of thirteen, however, young Friedrich was sent by his father to a military academy, and he suffered inexpressibly from the draconian measures imposed on him there. Like the youthful Nietzsche, he was assailed by all kinds of illnesses, and he was virtually unable to concentrate. He spent weeks at a time in the infirmary, and finally ended up among the pupils with the poorest grades. His academic failure was attributed to his illnesses. No one realized that it was the inhuman and absurd discipline imposed on him at this boarding school, where he spent eight years of his life, that completely exhausted his physical and mental energies. He found no other way of expressing his distress than the language of illness, the mute language of his own body, disregarded and misunderstood by everyone for centuries after.

This is Burschell's description of the school:

Here, in his most impressionable years, the young, freedom-loving boy was bound to feel like a prisoner, for the gates of the institution only opened for the obligatory walk guarded over by military chaperones. In all these eight years, Schiller had scarcely one single day to himself and only occasionally an hour or two in which he could do as he liked. School holidays were unknown at the time, leave of absence was unheard-of. The entire course of the day was subject to military regulation. The pupils slept in huge dormitories and were roused at five in the summer and six in the winter. Junior officers supervised the making of the beds and personal grooming. Then the pupils marched into the drill hall for morning roll call, proceeding from there to the refectory for breakfast, consisting of bread and gruel. Everything was done on command, be it the folding of hands for prayer, sitting down, or falling out. Lessons took place from seven till midday. Then came the half hour that earned young Schiller constant reprimands and the reputation of being a "pig": the period set aside for personal grooming, known as *propreté*. The pupils donned full military attire, the pale blue coat with the black cuffs, a white waistcoat and white breeches, turndown boots and rapier, the three-cornered hat with its trimmings and plumes. As the Duke [the founder of this school] could not stand red hair, Schiller had to powder it. Like all the others, he wore a long, artificial pigtail and two *papillotes* [curlers] at his temples, affixed with plaster. Thus attired, the pupils marched off first to midday roll call and then to the refectory. After the meal came first the obligatory walk and then military drill, followed by lessons from two to six, and subsequently the *propreté* process all over again. The rest of the day was devoted to personal study in accordance with a strict plan. Immediately after the evening meal, the pupils were sent to bed. Young Schiller remained trapped in the straitjacket of this unchanging routine until he was twenty-one years old.[1]

Schiller suffered repeatedly from extremely painful convulsions and cramps in many parts of his body. When he reached his forties, he developed a number of severe illnesses that constantly forced him to confront his fear of death. They were bound up with fits of delirium and finally killed him at the age of forty-six.

To my mind, there can be no doubt that these cramps and convulsions are attributable to the frequent administration of corporal punishment in his childhood and the cruel discipline he was subjected to in his later formative years. Properly speaking, his imprisonment began before he attended the military academy, at the hands of his father. In the name of self-discipline, this man rigorously and systematically suppressed any expression of pleasure or joy, both in his son and in himself. For example, the children were told to leave the table immediately if they felt any pleasure in whatever it was they were eating. And their father did precisely the same. This bizarre concern to quell anything in the nature of what we might call "quality of life" may have been something peculiar to Schiller's father. But the military academy system was widespread at the time, and it was upheld as the epitome of strict Prussian education. Little thought was given to what consequences it might have. The cruel surveillance system it involved recalls some of the descriptions we have of the Nazi concentration camps. While the state-organized sadism in those camps was undoubtedly even more vile and cruel than in the military academies, these institutions shared the same roots in the educational system prevalent in former centuries.[2] Both the commanding officers and the immediate perpetrators of these planned cruelties had had firsthand experience in their youth of beatings and various other methods of humiliation. They had learned them so well that they were later able to inflict them unthinkingly and without compunction on other individuals they had power over, such as children or prisoners. Schiller felt no urge to avenge himself on others for the horrors he had been exposed to. But his body was racked by suffering all his life as a result of the brutality he had to endure in childhood.

Of course, Schiller was no exception. Millions of men went through such schools as children, and they all had to learn to yield to the power of authority if they did not want to be severely punished or even killed. These experiences were instrumental in their unswerving allegiance to the Fourth Commandment, and the one thing they drummed into their children's heads was never on any account to call the authority of that commandment into question. Small wonder, then, that even today the great-great-grandchildren of those children still claim that a good beating from time to time never did them any harm.

But in a certain sense Schiller is, of course, an exception. Throughout all his works, from *The Robbers* to *William Tell*, we find a passionate revolt against the exercise of blind force by the authorities, and the sublime eloquence of the language in which that revolt is couched has given many people the courage to hope that someday this revolt might be successful. But none of these works contain the slightest indication of any knowledge on Schiller's part that his revolt against the absurd decrees of established authority was fueled by the early experiences stored in his body. His sufferings at the hands of his frightening, power-crazed father drove him to write. But he could not recognize the motivation behind that urge. His sole aim was to produce great and lasting literature. He sought to express the truth he found embodied in historical figures, and he achieved that aim with outstanding success. But the whole truth about the way he suffered at the hands of his father finds no mention. This suffering remained a closed book to him, all the way up to his early death.

It remained a mystery both to him and to the society of theater-goers and readers that has admired him for centuries and chosen him as an example to live up to because of his espousal of the cause of liberty and truth in his works. But that truth was not the whole truth, merely the truth acknowledged as such by society. How alarmed that same courageous Friedrich von Schiller would have been if someone had said to him, "You don't need to honor your father. People who have done you such harm do not deserve your love or respect, even if they are your parents. The price you pay for such filial devotion is appalling, the terrible physical torments you repeatedly go through. You can free yourself of them if you no longer obey the Fourth Commandment."

What would Schiller have said to that?

3

The Betrayal of Memory

Virginia Woolf

TWENTY YEARS AGO, in *Thou Shalt Not Be Aware: Society's Betrayal of the Child*, I discussed the life of Virginia Woolf, who, like her sister, Vanessa Bell, was sexually abused by her two half-brothers when she was a child and later apparently until adolescence.[1] In her diary, which ran to twenty-four volumes, Woolf constantly returned to that terrible period, in which she did not dare to confide in her parents because she knew she could expect no support from them. All her life she suffered from recurrent depression and yet still found the strength to work on her novels, hoping in this way to express her pain and ultimately to overcome the traumas of her childhood and adolescence. But in 1941 her depression gained the upper hand and Virginia Woolf drowned herself.

According to one of her biographers, Louise DeSalvo, Woolf began to doubt the authenticity of her own memories after reading the works of Freud, although she had already noted them in a memoir and knew that her sister had also been sexually abused by their half-brothers. DeSalvo thinks that from that point on Woolf followed the theories of Freud, ceasing to regard human behavior as the logical consequence of childhood experiences and instead seeing it as a result of drives, fantasies, and wishful thinking. DeSalvo assumed that Freud's writings plunged Woolf into total confusion. On the one hand, she knew exactly what had happened; on the other, she wished, like almost all victims of sexual abuse, that it had never been the case. Finally she gladly accepted Freud's theories and sacrificed her memories in the service of this denial. She began to idealize her parents even more and to describe her whole family in a roseate light, something she had never done before. After conceding that Freud was right, she became uncertain of herself, and confused, and she finally believed herself to be insane.

DeSalvo is convinced that this turn in Woolf's thinking reinforced her decision to kill herself, that her acceptance of Freud took away the foundation for the cause-and-effect relationship she had attempted to establish, thus forcing her to retract her own explanations for her bouts of depression and her mental state. Previously, Woolf attributed her depressive states to her terrible, humiliating experiences of sexual molestation. But if she followed Freud's theories, then there had to be other explanations. Perhaps her memories were distorted, not to say false; perhaps they were a reflection not of actual experience but of the projection of her own desires. Perhaps, in short, the whole business had been a product of her imagination.[2]

I do not doubt that reading Freud's work could have had an influence on Virginia Woolf, but I think that this may have been only a trigger and not the final cause of her suicide. We know that there were many such attempts long before Virginia could read Freud, the first one at the age of thirteen. Freud's work might have deepened her confusion but it represented only what society did and still does when faced with facts of scandalous sexual exploitation well hidden by families: it blames the victim and protects the adult persecutor. For that reason Woolf was totally alone with her monstrous history, in spite of so many good friends. The "care" she received from her family and from her husband, Leonard, was accompanied by lies and hypocrisy that she refused to see. She was free to question such attitudes in her novels but her own family remained sacrosanct. Woolf unques-tionably wanted to believe that she was loved—that the silence and indifference she endured was, in fact, love. As a result, she lived with such lies, and instead of facing the truth she blamed herself. She went on behaving in this way even after her suicide attempt in 1913, which occurred after she read how her own husband had defamed her in his novel *The Wise Virgins*. She then apologized for having caused *him* trouble.

Can we say that she had no courage? No, we can't; she showed more courage than most people in denouncing lies, but her fam-ily could not come to terms with such honesty. This is not sur-prising. The little girl continued to live in an adult woman's body, fearing her molesting half-brothers and her beloved parents, who remained silent. Had she been able to listen to her body, the true Virginia would certainly have spoken up. In order to do so, how-ever, she needed someone to say to her: "Open your eyes! They didn't protect you when you were in danger of losing your health and your mind, and now they refuse to see what has been done to you. How can you love them so much after all that?" No one offered that kind of support. Nor can anyone stand up to that kind of abuse alone, not even Virginia Woolf.

Malcolm Ingram, the noted lecturer in psychological medicine, believed that Woolf's "mental illness" had nothing to do with her childhood experiences, and her illness was genetically inherited from her family. Here is his opinion as quoted on the Virginia Woolf Web site:

> As a child she was sexually abused, but the extent and duration is difficult to establish. At worst she may have been sexually harassed and abused from the age of twelve to twenty-one by her [half-]brother George Duckworth, [fourteen] years her senior, and sexually exploited as early as six by her other [half-] brother . . .
>
> It is unlikely that the sexual abuse and her manic-depressive illness are related. However tempting it may be to relate the two, it must be more likely that, whatever her upbringing, her family history and genetic makeup were the determining factors in her mood swings *rather than her unhappy childhood* [italics added]. More relevant in her childhood experience is the long history of bereavements that punctuated her adolescence and precipitated her first depressions.[3]

Ingram's text goes against my own interpretation and ignores a large volume of literature that deals with trauma and the effects of childhood abuse. Here we see how people minimize the importance of information that might cause pain or discomfort— such as childhood abuse—and blame psychiatric disorders on family history instead. Woolf must have felt keen frustration when seemingly intelligent and well-educated people attributed her condition to her mental history, denying the effects of significant childhood experiences. In the eyes of many she remained a woman possessed by "madness." Nevertheless, the key to her condition lay tantalizingly close to the surface, so easily attainable, and yet neglected.

I think that Woolf's suicide could have been prevented if she had had an enlightened witness with whom she could have shared her feelings about the horrors inflicted on her at such an early age. But there was no one to turn to, and she considered Freud to be the expert on psychic disorders. Here she made a tragic mistake. His writings cast her into a state of severe uncertainty, and she preferred to despair of her own self rather than doubt the great father figure Sigmund Freud, who represented, as did her family, the system of values upheld by society, especially at the time.

UNFORTUNATELY, THESE STANDARDS have not changed greatly in the years since. As recently as 1987, journalist Nikolaus Frank remarked in an interview with the German magazine *Stern* that he could never forgive his father for the cruelties he had meted out to him. The public outcry caused by this statement was remarkable. In the war, Frank's father had been a *gauleiter* in Kraków and was responsible for the unspeakable sufferings inflicted on very many people. But society expected his son to be indulgent toward this monster. Nikolaus Frank received letters saying that the worst thing his father had done was to produce a son like him.

4

Self-Hatred and Unfulfilled Love

Arthur Rimbaud

ARTHUR RIMBAUD, whose paroxysms of brilliant, erotic verse electrified the late nineteenth century like no other poet of his generation, was born in 1854 and died of cancer in 1891, a few months after his right leg had been amputated. In other words, he lived to be only thirty-seven years old. Yves Bonnefoy, today's most esteemed French poet, tells us that Rimbaud's mother was harsh and brutal, a fact on which all the available sources are unanimous.

In his book *Rimbaud*, Bonnefoy describes her as ambitious, proud, stubbornly self-opinionated, arid, and full of covert hatred. He calls her the classic case of someone fired by the pure energy derived from bigoted religiosity. The astonishing letters she wrote around 1900 reveal that she was enamored of death and destruction. She was fascinated by graveyards, and at the age of seventy-five she had gravediggers lower her into the grave she was later to share with her dead children, Vitali and Arthur, so that she could have a foretaste of the eternal night that was to come.[1]

What must it have been like for an intelligent and sensitive child to grow up in the care of a woman like this? We find the answer in Rimbaud's poetry. Bonnefoy tells us that Mme. Rimbaud did everything in her power to curb and thwart her son's development as a poet, albeit to no avail. Failing that, she nipped in the bud every desire for independence on his part, every premonition of liberty. The boy took to regarding himself as an orphan, and his relationship to his mother diverged into hatred on the one hand, and obsequious dependency on the other. As a result of the fact that he received no token of affection, Rimbaud concluded that he must be in some way guilty: "With all the strength of his innocence, he rebelled fiercely against the judgment passed on him by his mother."[2]

Rimbaud's mother maintained total control over her children and called this control motherly love. Her acutely perceptive son saw through this lie. He realized that her constant concern for outward appearances had nothing to do with love. But he was unable to admit to this observation without reserve, because as a child he needed love, or at least the illusion of it. He could not hate his mother, particularly as she was so obviously concerned for him. So he hated himself instead, unconsciously convinced that in some obscure way he must have deserved such mendacity and coldness. Plagued by an ill-defined sense of disgust, he projected it onto the provincial town where he lived, onto the hypocrisy of the system of morality he grew up in (much like his contemporary Nietzsche in this respect), and onto himself. All his life he strove to escape these feelings, resorting in the process to alcohol, hashish, absinthe, opium, and extensive travels to far-away places. In his youth he made two attempts to run away from home but was caught and restored to his mother's "care" on both occasions.

His poetry reflects not only his self-hatred but also his quest for the love so completely denied him in the early stages of his life. Later, at school, he was fortunate enough to encounter a kindly teacher who gave him the companionship and support he so desperately needed in the decisive years of puberty. His teacher's affection and confidence enabled Rimbaud to write and to develop his philosophical ideas. But his childhood retained its stifling grip on him. He attempted to combat his despair at the absence of love in his life by transforming it into philosophical observations on the nature of true love. But these ideas were no more than abstractions because, despite his intellectual rejection of conventional morality, his emotional allegiance to the code of conduct it prescribed was unswerving. Self-disgust was legitimate, but detesting his mother was unthinkable. He could not pay heed to the painful messages of his childhood memories without destroying the hopes that had helped him to survive as a child. Time and again, Rimbaud tells us that he had no one to rely on except himself. This was surely the fruit of his experience with a mother who had nothing to offer him but her own derangement and hypocrisy, rather than true love. His entire life was a magnificent but vain attempt to save himself from destruction at the hands of his mother, with all the means at his disposal.

Young people who have gone through much the same kind of childhood as Rimbaud are often fascinated by his poetry because they can vaguely sense the presence of a kindred spirit in it.

Rimbaud's friendship with Paul Verlaine is well known in literary history. His longing for love and genuine communication initially appeared to find gratification in this friendship. But the mistrust rooted in his childhood gradually poisoned their intimacy, and this, coupled with Verlaine's own difficult past, prevented the love between them from achieving any permanence. Ultimately, their recourse to drugs made it impossible for them to live the life of total honesty that they were in search of. Their relationship was crippled by the psychological injuries they inflicted on each other. In the last resort, Verlaine acted in just as destructive a way as Rimbaud's mother, and the final crisis came when Rimbaud was shot by the drunken Verlaine, who was sentenced to two years in prison for his crime.

To salvage the genuine love he was deprived of in childhood, Rimbaud turned to the idea of love embodied in Christian charity and in understanding and compassion for others. He set out to give others what he himself had never received. He tried to understand his friend and to help Verlaine understand himself, but the repressed emotions from his childhood repeatedly interfered with this attempt. He sought redemption in Christian charity, but his implacably perspicacious intelligence would allow him no self-deception. Thus he spent his whole life searching for his own truth, but it remained hidden to him because he had learned at a very early age to hate himself for what his mother had done to him. He experienced himself as a monster, his homosexuality as a vice (this was easy to do given Victorian attitudes toward homosexuality), his despair as a sin. But not once did he allow himself to direct his endless, justified rage at the true culprit, the woman who had kept him locked up in her prison for as long as she could. All his life he attempted to free himself of that prison, with the help of drugs, travel, illusions, and above all poetry. But in all these desperate efforts to open the doors that would have led to liberation, one of them remained obstinately shut, the most important one: the door to the emotional reality of his childhood, to the feelings of the little child who was forced to grow up with a severely disturbed, malevolent woman, with no father to protect him from her.

Rimbaud's biography is a telling instance of how the body cannot but seek desperately for the early nourishment it has been denied. Rimbaud was driven to assuage a deficiency, a hunger that could never be stilled. His drug addiction, his compulsive travels, and his friendship with Verlaine can be interpreted not merely as attempts to flee from his mother, but also as a quest for the nourishment she had withheld from him. As his internal reality inevitably remained unconscious, Rimbaud's life was marked by compulsive repetition. After every abortive escape attempt, he returned to his mother, doing so both after the separation from Verlaine and at the end of his life, when he had finally sacrificed his creative gifts by giving up his writing to become a businessman, thus indirectly fulfilling his mother's expectations of him. Although Rimbaud spent the last days of his life in a hospital in Marseille, he had gone back to western France immediately before that, where he was looked after by his mother and sister. The quest for his mother's love ended in the prison of childhood.

5

The Imprisoned Child and the
Necessity of Denying Pain

Yukio Mishima

L IKE RIMBAUD, the famous Japanese writer Yukio
Mishima, who committed hara-kiri in 1970 at the age of
forty-five, often spoke of himself as a monster because he
felt within him an inclination toward things morbid and perverted. His fantasies revolved around death, the dark side of the
world, and sexual violence. On the other hand, his poems indicate
an unusual sensitivity that caused him immense suffering, suffering that derived from the tragic experiences of his childhood.

Mishima was his parents' first child. When he was born, in
1925, they were newly married and living in his grandparents'
house—there was nothing unusual about this in Japan at the
time. Almost from the very beginning he was quartered in the
room of his fifty-year-old grandmother. His cot stood next to her
bed, and he lived there for years, cut off from the outside
world and exposed exclusively to her needs. Mishima's grand-

mother suffered from severe depression. Occasionally she alarmed the boy with outbreaks of hysteria. She had nothing but contempt for her husband and for her son, Mishima's father, but in her own way she worshipped her little grandson and wanted him to belong to her and no one else. In his autobiography, Mishima recalls the oppressiveness and the fetid smell of the room he shared with his grandmother. But he tells us nothing of any rage or revulsion that he felt about his situation, because it appeared normal to him. At the age of four, he developed a severe illness, diagnosed as "self-intoxication," which later proved to be chronic. When he first went to school, at the age of six, it was the very first time he had had any contact with other children, and he felt strange and alien in their midst. Naturally enough, he had difficulty relating to these other children, who were emotionally more uninhibited and spontaneous, since they had experienced entirely different treatment and surroundings in their own families. When he was nine, his parents moved into an apartment of their own, but they did not take their son with them. It was at this time that he started writing poems, actively and enthusiastically encouraged by his grandmother. When he finally moved in with his parents, at the age of twelve, his mother was proud of what he had written, but his father tore up the manuscripts, and Mishima was forced to carry on writing in secret. At home he found neither understanding nor encouragement. His grandmother had tried to make a girl out of him, whereas his father attempted to turn him into a "real man," which involved severe beatings. As a result he frequently visited his grandmother, who represented a refuge from the cruelty of his father. Around this time, she took him on his first visit to the theater. This opened the door to a whole new world: the world of feelings.

I understand Mishima's suicide as the expression of his inability to experience his early feelings of revolt against, anger toward, and indignation at the behavior of his grandmother. This inability was a direct result of the gratitude he felt toward her. In his loneliness, and in comparison to the way his father behaved, his grandmother was bound to appear to him as a savior figure. His true feelings remained pent up in the prison of his attachment to this woman, who exploited the child from the outset for the gratification of her needs, including (presumably) her sexual cravings. But his biographers draw a veil of silence over all this, and right to the very end Mishima himself made no reference to it. He never faced up to his own truth.

All kinds of reasons have been advanced to explain Mishima's hara-kiri. But the most convincing reason is hardly ever mentioned. After all, it is quite normal for us to owe a debt of gratitude to our parents and grandparents (or the people standing in for them), even if the treatment we experienced at their hands was sheer unadulterated torture. This is an integral part of morality, as we understand it. But it is a species of morality that consigns our genuine feelings and our own personal truth to an unmarked grave. Severe illnesses, early death, and suicide are the logical consequence of subjection to the laws that we call morality, although in fact they suffocate our true lives. This will continue to be the case, all over the world, as long as we show greater reverence to these laws than to life itself. The body rebels against such treatment, but the only language at its command is the language of illness, a language that is rarely understood as long as the denial of true feelings in childhood remains unrecognized.

Many of the Ten Commandments can still claim validity today. But the Fourth Commandment is diametrically opposed to the laws of psychology. It is imperative that there be general recognition of the fact that enforced "love" can do a very great deal of harm. People who were loved in childhood will love their parents in return. There is no need of a commandment to tell them to do so. Obeying a commandment can never be the basis for love.

6

Suffocated by Mother's Love

Marcel Proust

WHOEVER HAS TAKEN the (very considerable) time needed to immerse oneself in the world of Marcel Proust knows what a wealth of feeling, sensitivity, imagery, and observation this author has lavished on his readers. To write as he did, he must have experienced this wealth of impressions as he worked, year after year, on his great novel *In Search of Lost Time*. Why did these experiences not give him the strength to live? Why did he die only two months after completing the book? And why of suffocation? The conventional answer is Because he had asthma and a bout of pneumonia was enough to kill him. But why did he have asthma? He suffered his first severe attack when he was nine. What drove him into this disease? Did he not have a loving mother? Was he able to sense that love, or was he assailed by doubts?

The fact is that he could describe the observations, feelings, and thoughts that constitute his own special world only after his mother had died. Occasionally, he felt that he was an intolerable burden for her. He could never reveal himself to her as he really was, with all the things he thought and felt. This emerges clearly in his letters to his mother, from which I quote below. In her own way, she "loved" him. She was greatly concerned for his health and well-being, but at the same time she wanted complete control over him and dictated his relationships, attempting even when he was eighteen to thwart those that she felt to be undesirable for him. She wanted him to be the way she needed him to be, dependent and docile. While he occasionally resisted this interference, he at the same time meekly, and sometimes desperately, apologized for his disobedience, so much did he fear losing her affection. Although he sought her love all his life, he had to protect himself by inwardly withdrawing from her constant control and her claims to power over him.

Proust's asthma was an expression of this dilemma. He breathed in too much air (love) and was not allowed to exhale the superfluous air (control)—that is, to rebel against his mother's engulfing claims. True, his magnificent, seven-volume novel enabled him to express himself and to bestow a gift of unusual generosity on his readers. But for years he suffered physical torment because he could not afford to face up totally and consciously to the suffering inflicted on him by his overpowering, dominant, and demanding mother. Right to the very end, his main concern was to spare the feelings of his internalized mother, and he also believed that he must protect himself from the truth. His body was unable to accept this uneasy compromise. It knew the truth, probably from birth. For Marcel's body, his mother's manipulation and overwhelming concern were never an expression of genuine love, but a token of fear. It was, in all probability, the fear felt by a conventionally minded, obedient daughter from a "good" bourgeois family in the face of her son's extraordinary creative powers. Jeanne Proust was greatly concerned to live up to the expectations involved in being the wife of a revered physician and professor and to be respected by the members of a social class whose approval was very important to her. She experienced Marcel's originality and vitality as a threat, one that she set out to combat with all the means at her disposal. This did not escape her sensitive, perceptive son. But he had to keep his own counsel for a very long time. Only after his mother's death did he succeed in publishing his acute observations and criticizing the bourgeois society of the day with an acuteness equaled by hardly anyone else before him. His own mother was spared this criticism, although she herself was the very incarnation of the mentality it was leveled at.

At the age of thirty-four, immediately after the death of his mother, Proust wrote to his friend Comte Robert de Montesquiou:

> She knows that I am incapable of living without her. . . . From now on, my life has lost its sole purpose, its only sweetness, its only love, its only solace. I have lost the one whose unending vigilance gave me the only manna of my life, in peace, and in love. . . . I am drenched with pain. . . . As the nurse who looked after her said: In her eyes, I was always four years old.[1]

This description of Proust's love for his mother faithfully reflects his tragically dependent attachment to her, which brooked no liberation and left him no scope for open resistance to her permanent surveillance. His asthma was an expression of this dilemma: "I breathe in so much air but I must not breathe it out again, everything she gives me *must* be good for me, even if it stifles me."

A look back at Proust's childhood casts light on the origins of this tragedy. It explains why he was inextricably bound up with his mother for so long and could not free himself of her influence, although he undoubtedly suffered as a result.

Proust's parents were married on September 3, 1870. Their first son, Marcel, was born in Auteuil on July 10, 1871, in the course of a night full of clamor and uproar caused by the fact that the population was still reeling from the shock of the Prussian invasion of France. It is easy to imagine that his mother was hardly able to free herself from the nervous tension prevailing at the time and to concentrate her loving attentions exclusively on her newborn baby. It is also fair to assume that the baby's body sensed this disquiet and began to harbor doubts about whether he was welcome or not. In this situation, the child would certainly have required greater reassurance than he was given. In some babies, such a deficiency can easily cause mortal fear that later imposes an immense strain on their childhood. This was probably the case with Marcel.

Throughout his childhood, he could not go to sleep at night unless his mother had given him a good-night kiss, and the more this compulsive need was felt by his parents—and indeed by everyone else around him—to be an embarrassing instance of "bad behavior," the more imperative it became. Like every child, Marcel wanted nothing more dearly than to believe in his mother's love, but somehow he appeared to be incapable of detaching himself from the memory stored in his body, reminding him of his mother's mixed feelings immediately after his birth. He needed the good-night kiss to blot out that initial, all-powerful physical perception. But the very next night the doubts were back. Also, the constant stream of visitors in the salon downstairs may have aroused in the child's mind the suspicion that all these men and women of the haute bourgeoisie meant more to his mother than he did. After all, how small and insignificant he was in comparison! So there he lay in his bed, waiting for the token of love he so desperately desired. But what he received from his mother instead were constant admonitions to be well-mannered, well-adjusted, "normal."

Later, as an adult, Marcel set out to explore the world that, in his view, had stolen his mother's love from him. He did this initially with the help of his firsthand experience as a society dandy, later, after his mother's death, in his imagination, describing this world with unprecedented passion, precision, and sensitivity. It is as if he had embarked on a long journey in search of an answer to the questions that tormented him: "Mother, why are all these people more interesting than I am? Do you not recognize their hollowness, their snobbery? Why does my life, my longing for you, my love for you count for so little? Why am I no more than a nuisance?"

The child might indeed have expressed himself thus if he had been able to consciously experience his emotions. But Marcel wanted to be a good boy and not cause any problems. So he made his way into his mother's world, and this world began to fascinate him. Poetic license enabled him to portray it as he thought fit, and he could also criticize it freely. He did all this from his bed. It was here that he undertook his imaginary journeys, as if the sickbed were a sanctuary protecting him from the consequences of his merciless dissection and the reprisals he feared so much.

Through the figures in his novels a writer can express genuine feelings that he would never articulate to his parents in reality. In his early, strongly autobiographical novel *Jean Santeuil*, published posthumously and drawn upon by biographer Claude Mauriac as a source of information on Proust's early years, we find the author addressing his own personal dilemma much more directly, giving us to understand that he has indeed registered the rejection by his parents. He speaks of "great opportunities for unhappiness . . . in the nature of this son, in the state of his health, his melancholy inclinations, his wastefulness, his inertia, the impossibility for him to find a place in life" and of "the squandering of his intellectual gifts."[2] In the same novel, he tells us of his revolt against his mother, but only in the guise of his hero, Jean:

> His anger at himself increased his anger at his parents. But as they were the cause of his anxiety, his cruel inactivity, his fits of sobbing, his migraine, and his insomnia, he would gladly have done something to harm them, or, better still, instead of receiving his mother with imprecations when she came in, have told her that he had no intention of working, that he would spend every night somewhere else, that he considered his father a blockhead . . . and all this merely because he felt the need to lash out indiscriminately and, with words that struck home like blows, pay back something of the evil she had done to him. But these words that he could not utter remained pent up inside and acted like a poison that lodges itself in the body and gradually permeates every extremity. His hands and feet trembled, he clutched convulsively at the air, seeking for prey.[3]

But after his mother's death, all we find are declarations of love. What has become of his true life, with its doubts and strong feelings? It was all transformed into art, and the price for this flight from reality was asthma.

In a letter to his mother, dated March 9,1903, Proust writes: "But I lay no claim to joy. I have long since renounced it."[4] And in December 1903: "But at least I conjure the night with plans for a life in accordance with your will," and later in the same letter: "For I would prefer to have these attacks and please you, rather than displease you and not have them."[5] Highly significant for the conflict between morality and the body is the following passage from a letter written in early December 1902: "The truth is that as soon as I feel well, you destroy everything until I feel bad again, because the life that gives me relief provokes you to anger. . . . But it is saddening that I cannot have your affection and my health at the same time."[6]

The famous episode of the madeleine from *In Search of Lost Time*, in fact, relates one of the rare moments of happiness in which Proust felt safe and secure in the presence of his mother. As an eleven-year-old boy, he returned from a walk, wet and cold, and was hugged by his mother and given hot tea and a madeleine. No recriminations. This was obviously enough to relieve the child for a while of the mortal fears slumbering inside him, probably since birth, and bound up with his uncertainty about whether his parents really wanted him.

These latent fears were constantly revived by the frequent reprimands and criticisms addressed to him by his parents. The intelligent child may have thought, "Mother, I am a nuisance to you. You would like me to be different from the way I am. You show me this all the time, and you tell me so as well." As a child

Marcel was unable to express this in words, and the causes of his fears remained hidden from everyone. He lay alone in his room, waiting for some proof of his mother's love and an explanation of why she wanted him to be different. This fact hurt. The pain was obviously too strong to be felt, and his inquiries and doubts were stamped as "literary" and banished to the realm of art. Marcel Proust was denied the chance to decipher the enigma of his life. I believe that the quest for "lost time" in the title of his great novel was the quest for the life he never lived.

In fairness, it has to be said that Proust's mother was no worse than the average mother of her day, and in her own way she was certainly concerned for her son's well-being. But I cannot concur with the chorus of biographers who praise her maternal qualities to the utmost, the reason being that I find it impossible to identify with their system of values. One of them writes, for example, that Jeanne was an outstanding example of the virtue of self-sacrifice and successfully transmitted this to her son. It may well be that Proust learned from his mother to deny himself any enjoyment or zest in life, but I do not consider such an attitude either praiseworthy or virtuous.

What caused Proust's severe physical condition was the obligation of undying gratitude and the impossibility of putting up any resistance to the mother's controls and restrictions. It was internalized morality that forced Marcel Proust to suppress his rebellion.

If he had ever been able to address to his mother the words that he puts into the mouth of his hero Jean Santeuil, then he would not have developed asthma, he would not have suffered from attacks of suffocating breathlessness, he would not have had to spend half his life in bed, and he would not have died so young. He puts this quite clearly in the letter to his mother, in which he says that he would rather be ill than run the risk of displeasing her. Even today, statements of this kind are by no means rare. What we need to do is to make it clear to ourselves what consequences such emotional blindness entails.

7

A Past Master at Splitting Off Feelings

James Joyce

J AMES JOYCE HAD to undergo many eye operations. What was it that he was not allowed to see or feel? After his father's death, he wrote in a letter to Harriet Shaw Weaver, dated January 17, 1932:

> My father had an extraordinary affection for me. He was the silliest man I ever knew and yet cruelly shrewd. He thought of and talked of me up to his last breath. I was very fond of him always, being a sinner myself, and even liked his faults. Hundreds of pages and scores of characters in my books came from him. His dry (or rather wet) wit and his expression of face often convulsed me with laughter.[1]

In contrast to this idealized portrait of his father, here is James Joyce's letter to his wife on August 29, 1904, shortly after his mother's death:

How could I like the idea of home? . . . My mother was slowly killed, I think, by my father's ill-treatment, by years of trouble, and by my cynical frankness of conduct. When I looked on her face as she lay in her coffin—a face grey and wasted with cancer—I understood that I was looking on the face of a victim and I cursed the system which had made her a victim.* We were seventeen in family. My brothers and sisters are nothing to me. One brother alone is capable of understanding me.[2]

How much suffering is there hidden behind these matter-of-fact lines, the suffering of the eldest son of a mother of seventeen children and a violent alcoholic? This suffering is not expressed in Joyce's works; instead we find him fending it off with the aid of brilliantly provocative prose. The father's antics were admired by the frequently beaten child and transformed into literature by the adult writer. I attribute the great success of his novels to the fact that very many people admire and appreciate this particular form of emotional defense, both in literature and in life. In *The Truth Will Set You Free*, I have discussed this phenomenon with reference to Frank McCourt's memoir *Angela's Ashes*.

---

* The system, not the idealized father! —AM

Postscript to Part I

THERE ARE INDEED countless other people who have
been through similar experiences, but the authors whose
life traumas I have just discussed are world famous, so
the truth of what I have to say about them can be verified by consulting their works and their biographies. What they all have in
common is their unswerving allegiance to the Fourth Commandment. They all honored their parents throughout their lives, even
though those parents did them immeasurable harm. They sacrificed the desire for truth, self-loyalty, genuine communication,
understanding, and appreciation on the altar of parental respect,
all in the hope of being loved and not rejected. The truth that
found its way into their works was disassociated from themselves. This was the burden imposed by the Fourth Commandment, and it kept them penned up in the prison of denial.

This denial led to severe illnesses and premature death,

another indication of how wrong Moses was when he said that honoring one's parents meant that one would live longer. The Fourth Commandment very clearly utters a threat.

Of course, we cannot deny the fact that many people live for a long time even though they idealize the parents who were once cruel to them. But we do not know how they contrived to come to terms with their own un-truth. Most of them passed it on unconsciously to the next generation. What we do know is that, at some point, the writers we have been discussing began to suspect their own truth. But isolated in a society that will always take the part of the parents, they were unable to find the courage to abandon their denial.

Just how strong this social pressure can be is something that each and every one of us can experience for ourselves. Adults realizing that they were cruelly treated by their mothers in childhood and talking openly and frankly about that fact will invariably get the same response, from therapists as much as anyone else: "Yes, but she had a difficult time of it, and she did a lot for you. You shouldn't condemn her; you shouldn't see things in black and white and take a one-sided view of things. There's no such thing as ideal parents, etc." The impression we get is that the people who talk in this way are, in fact, defending their own mothers, though the person they are speaking to is not attacking them. This social pressure is much stronger than we tend to realize.

So I hope very much that my discussion of these writers will not be understood as a criticism of their lack of courage. It is meant rather as a sympathetic portrayal of the tragedy of people unable in their isolation to admit their own personal truth, although they sensed it deep down in their own selves. I am writing this book in the hope of being able to reduce that isolation. In therapy, it is by no means unusual to encounter the loneliness of the small child that the adult once was. After all, therapy itself is usually conducted in a way that is also dictated by the Fourth Commandment.

The Internal World

II

TRADITIONAL MORALITY IN THERAPY AND THE KNOWLEDGE OF THE BODY

Without memories of childhood,
it is as if you were doomed
to drag a big box around with you,
though you don't know what's in it.
And the older you get,
the heavier it becomes,
and the more impatient you are
to finally open the thing.
—*Jurek Becker**

* As a small boy, Jurek Becker was interned in the Ravensbrück and Sachsenhausen concentration camps. He had no memory whatsoever of them. He spent all his life in search of the little child who, thanks to his mother's care, survived those horrors of those camps.

THE WRITERS WE discussed in Part I all lived between the mid-eighteenth and the mid-twentieth centuries. What has changed in the meantime? Not much, basically, except for the fact that survivors of childhood abuse can now seek therapy in an attempt to free themselves from the consequences of that abuse. Frequently, however, not only the victims themselves but also their therapists are reluctant to square up to the truth of what happened to them in childhood. Accordingly, it is still very rare for that liberation process to be fully successful. If clients can actually experience their emotions, there may be a temporary alleviation of the symptoms. The emotions can be consciously felt, they can be expressed in another's presence, and this is something that has never been possible before. But as long as the therapist tacitly stands in the service of some "deity" (parental figure), she will hardly be able to help her clients find their way to genuine autonomy. The morality implicit in the Fourth Commandment will continue to hold sway over both of them, and the body will pay the price for this sacrifice.

If I assert, here and now, that this sacrifice is unnecessary, that one can free oneself of the dictatorship of conventional morality and the Fourth Commandment without having to punish oneself for it or do harm to others, some people may accuse me of naïve optimism. For how can I prove to someone that freedom is within reach, if all his life he has clung to the constraints that were necessary for his survival, and if he cannot imagine life without those constraints? I can say that I myself have achieved such freedom by getting to the bottom of my own story, but I have to admit that I am not a good example. After all, it took me over forty years to arrive at the stage I have reached now. But there are other examples. I know people who have succeeded in unearthing their memories in a much shorter space of time, and the discovery of their own truth has enabled them to emerge from the autistic hiding place that used to be their only refuge. In my case, the reason the journey took so long was that I was on my own for most of it. Only in the final stages did I seek and find the kind of therapeutic companionship I needed.

On that journey I encountered others who were also in search of their own stories. They wanted to understand what they had to protect themselves against, what it was that had caused them such fear, how those fears and the severe injuries inflicted on them in their early years had affected their whole lives. Much like myself, they had to assert themselves against the strictures of traditional morality. But they were not entirely alone. There were already books they could consult, groups they could turn to,

and this helped them in the process of liberation. Once their perceptions had been confirmed and corroborated, they were able to
break out of the state of confusion they had been trapped in and
allow themselves to admit their indignation and horror by gradually facing up to their own truth.

The playwright Henrik Ibsen used the phrase "pillars of
society" to refer to those people in positions of power who
profit from the mendacity of the society they live in. I hope
that those people who have recognized their own story and
freed themselves from the lies of conventional morality will be
the pillars of a future society built on conscious awareness.
Without the awareness of what happened to us at the outset of
our lives, the entire fabric of our culture seems to me to be
nothing other than a farce. Writers are concerned to produce
good literature. They make no attempt to recognize the unconscious sources of their creativity, of their urge for expression
and communication. Most of them fear that they would then
forfeit their ability to write. I have identified a similar reluc-
tance in many painters—even those whose works, in my eyes,
make clear reference to their unconscious fears: painters like
Francis Bacon, Hieronymus Bosch, Salvador Dalí, and countless other surrealists. In their work they do indeed make an
effort to communicate, but at a level that serves the denial of
their childhood experiences by calling itself art. One of the
major taboos operative in our engagement with art and literature is the tenet that artists' biographies should be left out of
account when we talk about their work. In my view, the things
that have happened to artists in their lives are precisely what
goads them on in their unflagging quest for new forms of
expression. Those events are consigned to oblivion both by the

artist and society, because otherwise they might reveal the early suffering caused by cruel upbringing.

Almost all the institutions established by society conspire to encourage this flight from the truth. After all, such institutions are run by people, and most people get alarmed when the word "childhood" is mentioned in their presence. We encounter this fear everywhere—in the consulting rooms of physicians, psychotherapists, and lawyers, in the law courts, and, last but not least, in the media.

The last time I paid a visit to my local bookshop, one of the saleswomen told me about a television program she had seen on the subject of child abuse. The show referred to some extreme cases of cruelty, including the deeds perpetrated by one mother who was a hospital nurse. She created the impression of an extremely concerned and loving mother to the pediatricians she consulted. But in her own home she deliberately used medical preparations to provoke illnesses in her children that ultimately killed them. In the initial stages at least, no one suspected any foul play. The woman in the bookshop was highly indignant that the experts taking part in the program had said nothing about the causes of such behavior. Instead, they appeared to imply that it was some stroke of fate, an act of God inflicted on these parents and their children for no apparent reason.

"Why didn't those experts tell the truth?" she asked me. "Why didn't they say that mothers like that were severely maltreated in their childhood, that their deeds are nothing but a repetition of things done to them long ago?"

I said, "If the experts knew that, they would say so. Obviously they don't."

"But how is that possible?" the woman insisted. "I know it, and

I'm no expert. All you need to do is read a few books. Since I started doing that, my relationship with my children has changed radically. So how can an expert tell us that fortunately such extreme cases of cruelty are rare, and there's nothing we can say about the causes?"

This woman's reaction made me realize that the time had come to write one more book—though it may take some time before it is understood by all those people it can help to find relief from their sufferings. But I have no doubt that, even now, there are many who, on the basis of their own experience, will be able to confirm the truth of what this book says.

MY ATTEMPTS TO persuade the Vatican of the importance of early childhood experiences have revealed how impossible it is to arouse feelings of compassion in men and women who right at the beginning of their lives learned to suppress their genuine, natural feelings so mercilessly that there is no trace of them left in their conscious minds. All curiosity about the feelings of others has been stifled. It seems that people who were psychically mutilated in early life immure themselves in a fortress deep inside themselves, where they can only pray to God. It is to Him that they delegate all their responsibility, and they carefully obey the precepts of the church so as not to be punished by this "loving" God for any sins of omission they might commit.

Shortly after the capture of Saddam Hussein in late 2003, the Vatican was largely instrumental in orchestrating the sudden increase, all over the world, of voices expressing compassion for the unscrupulous tyrant who had been such an object of fear and loathing while he was still at large. But in my view we cannot simply allow ourselves to base our judgment of tyrants on ordinary compassion for the individual, if that means disregarding the things they have done.

As biographers Judith Miller and Laurie Mylroie tell us in their 1990 book *Saddam Hussein and the Crisis in the Gulf*, Saddam Hussein was born on April 28, 1937. He grew up in a peasant family living in penury near Tikrit. They had no land of their own. His biological father died before his birth. His stepfather, a shepherd, constantly humiliated the boy, calling him "son of a whore" and "son of a bitch," beating him mercilessly and tormenting him in the most brutal way imaginable. To exploit young Saddam's working capacity to the full, he forbade him to go to school until the boy was ten. Instead, he would wake him in the middle of the night and tell him to guard the flocks. In these formative years, children develop an image of the world. Ideas take shape in their minds about the values that are worth upholding in life. At the same time, they begin to cherish desires and dream of their fulfillment. For Saddam, the slave of his stepfather, these desires all centered around one thing: limitless power over others. In his brain the idea presumably took shape that he could regain the human dignity he had been so radically deprived of only by possessing the same power over others that his stepfather had over him. Throughout his childhood, there were no other ideals, no other examples to live up to, only the omnipotent stepfather and himself, the defenseless victim of the terror inflicted on him. It was in line with this pattern that the adult Hussein later organized the structure of the country he ruled over. His body knew nothing but violence.

Every dictator denies the sufferings of his childhood and attempts to forget them by indulging his megalomania. But as the unconscious mind of an individual has completely registered his biography in the cells of the body, it will at some point urge that individual to confront the truth. After the coalition invasion, despite the immense financial resources at his disposal, Saddam sought refuge precisely in the vicinity of the place where he was born, the place where all help was denied him as a child, a highly precarious spot that could not provide any real protection. The fact that he should have chosen this place to "go to ground" reflects the desperate plight of his early years and clearly illustrates the power of compulsive repetition. His return to his childhood was the return to a place where he had no chance of escape.

There is conclusive evidence that the character of a tyrant will not change as long as he lives, that he will abuse his power in a destructive way as long as he encounters no resistance. The point is that his genuine aim, the unconscious aim concealed behind all his conscious activities, remains the same: to use his power to blot out the humiliations inflicted on him in childhood and denied by him ever since. But this aim can never be achieved. The past cannot be expunged, nor can one come to terms with it, as long as one denies the suffering it involved. Accordingly, a dictator's efforts to achieve that aim are doomed to failure. Compulsive repetition will always reassert itself. And an endless succession of victims is forced to pay the price.

With his own behavior, Hitler demonstrated to the world the kind of person his father was and the kind of treatment he suffered at his hands when he was a child: destructive, pitiless, ostentatious, merciless, boastful, perverted, self-enamored, shortsighted, and stupid. In his unconscious imitation he was faithful to his father's example. For the same reason, other dictators like Stalin, Mussolini, Franco, Ceausescu, Idi Amin, and

Saddam Hussein behaved in a very similar way. Saddam's biography is a striking example of how extreme humiliation in childhood is avenged on thousands and thousands of victims at a later date. The refusal to learn from these facts may be grotesque, but the reasons for that refusal are not difficult to identify.

The fact is that an unscrupulous tyrant mobilizes the suppressed fears and anxieties of those who were beaten as children but have never been able to accuse their own fathers of doing so. Their loyalty to these fathers is unswerving, despite the torments suffered at their hands. Every tyrant symbolizes such a father, the figure whom the abused children remain attached to with every fiber of their being, hoping that one day they will be able to transform him into a loving parent by remaining blind.

This hope may have been what prompted the representatives of the Roman Catholic Church to demonstrate their compassion for Hussein. In 2002, I turned to a number of cardinals for support when I presented the Vatican with material on the delayed effects of spanking and asked the authorities there to do what they could to enlighten young parents on this subject. As I have said, not one of the cardinals I approached with this request showed the slightest interest in the universally ignored but crucially important issue of physically abused children. Nor did I come across the slightest indication of Christian charity or compassion in connection with this issue. Today, however, those same representatives are eager to show that they are indeed capable of compassion. Significantly, however, this compassion is lavished not on maltreated children or on Saddam's victims but on Saddam himself, on the unscrupulous father figure that the feared despot symbolizes.

As a rule, beaten, tormented, and humiliated children who

have never received support from a helping witness later develop a high degree of tolerance for the cruelties perpetrated by parent figures and a remarkable indifference to the sufferings borne by children exposed to inhumane treatment. The last thing they wish to be told is that they themselves once belonged to the same group. Indifference is a way of preserving them from opening their eyes to reality. In this way they become advocates of evil, however convinced they may be of their humane intentions. From an early age they were forced to suppress and ignore their true feelings. They were forced to put their trust not in those feelings but solely in the regulations imposed on them by their parents, their teachers, and the church authorities. Now the tasks facing them in their adult lives leave them no time to perceive their own feelings, unless those feelings happen to fit in precisely with the patriarchal value system in which they live and which prescribes compassion for the father, however destructive and dangerous he may be. The more comprehensive a tyrant's catalogue of crimes is, the more he can count on tolerance, provided his admirers are hermetically closed off from access to the sufferings of their own childhood.

8

The Familiarity of Cruelty to Children

I N M Y R E A D I N G of the notes sent in to the "Our Childhood" forums* over the past few years, one thing has struck
me repeatedly. Most newcomers write that, while they have
been visiting the forum for some time, they have serious doubts
whether they have come to the right place because they themselves never really experienced abuse in childhood. Appalled by
the sufferings reported on there, they say that, although they
were occasionally beaten and exposed to contempt or other
forms of humiliation, they never had to suffer anything remotely
like the cruelties inflicted on many of the forum participants. In
the course of time, however, these newcomers also start reporting on shocking behavior on the part of their parents, behavior
that can be unreservedly classified as abuse and is also considered as such by the others. They need some time to actually feel

* Addresses can be found on my Web site, www.alice-miller.com.

the suffering they went through as children. Thanks to the sympathy of the other participants, they can gradually admit their true feelings.

This phenomenon is a reflection of the attitude displayed by the entire population of the world with regard to child abuse and cruelty to children. Such behavior is at best regarded as an involuntary "lapse from grace," committed by parents who, though they have the best intentions, are simply overtaxed from time to time by the burden of bringing up a child. In the same vein, unemployment or overwork are quoted as the reason that a father gives his children a slap, or marital tensions are cited as the reason a mother has beaten her children with a hanger until it breaks. Such absurd explanations are the fruits of the morality we live by, a system that has always taken the part of the adults and left the children to fend for themselves as best they may. From this perspective, it is of course impossible to perceive the sufferings of children for what they are. It was this realization that prompted me to set up these forums, where people can tell the story of what they have been through and in time, so I hope, reveal what a little child has to go through as long as he or she is deprived of support from society. These reports demonstrate how an extreme form of hatred can evolve. It is so strong that originally innocent children can later, in adulthood, put the insane fantasies of a madman into practice. They can organize, acclaim, support, defend, and finally forget something as monstrous as the Holocaust.

The inquiry into the childhood patterns, the abuse, and the humiliation that have contributed to turning normal children into monsters is still, however, a matter of public neglect. These monsters and the people who have directed their feelings of anger and rage against themselves and have fallen ill for that reason have one thing in common: they ward off any kind of accusation from the parents who once maltreated them so severely. They do not know what that treatment has done to them, they do not know how much they have suffered from it. Above all, they do not want to know. They see it as something beneficial, something inflicted on them for their own good.

Self-therapy manuals and the extensive literature on therapeutic care tell much the same story. Hardly anywhere do we find an author coming out squarely on the side of the child. Readers are advised to "snap out" of the role of victim, to stop blaming others for the things that have gone wrong in their lives, to be true to their own selves. This, they are told, is the only way of freeing themselves from the past and maintaining good relations with their parents. For me, such advice embodies the contradictions of poisonous pedagogy and of conventional morality. It is actively dangerous because it is very likely to leave the former victims in a state of confusion and moral uncertainty, so that the individuals in question may never be able to attain true adulthood throughout their whole lives.

True adulthood would mean no longer denying the truth. It would mean feeling the repressed suffering, consciously acknowledging the story remembered by the body at an emotional level, and integrating that story instead of repressing it. Whether contact with the parents can then in fact be maintained will depend on the given circumstances in each individual case. What is absolutely imperative is the termination of the harmful attachment to the *internalized* parents of childhood, an attachment that, though we call it love, certainly does not deserve the name. It is made up of different ingredients, such as gratitude, compassion, expectations, denial, illusions, obedience, fear, and the anticipation of punishment.

Time and again, I have asked myself why therapy works for some people while others remain the prisoners of their symptoms despite years of analysis or therapeutic care. In each and every case I examined, I was able to establish that when people found the kind of therapeutic care and companionship that enabled them to discover their own story and give free expression to their indignation at their parents' behavior, they were able to liberate themselves from the maltreated child's destructive attachment. As adults they were able to take their lives into their own hands and did not need to hate their parents. The opposite was the case with people whose therapists enjoined them to forgive and forget, actually believing that such forgiveness could have a salutary, curative effect. They remained trapped in the position of small children who believe they love their parents but in fact allow themselves to be controlled all their lives by the internalized parents and ultimately develop some kind of illness that leads to premature death. Such dependency *actively fosters the hatred* that, though repressed, remains active, and it drives them to direct their aggression at innocent people. We only hate as long as we feel totally powerless.

I have received hundreds of letters confirming this assertion. Paula, a twenty-six-year-old woman who suffered from various allergies, wrote saying that every time she visited her uncle when she was still a child he would subject her to sexual harassment, unashamedly fondling her breasts even in the presence of other members of the family. At the same time, this uncle was the only member of the family to pay any attention to the girl. No one protected or defended her. When she complained to her parents, they said she should not let him do it. Instead of standing by her, they foisted the responsibility for the whole affair onto the child.

When her uncle fell ill with cancer, Paula refused to visit him because of the fury and disgust the old man now inspired in her. But her therapist was convinced that she would regret this refusal later and that there was no point in arousing the animosity of her family at such a difficult time. It would not do her any good. Accordingly, Paula went to see him, swallowing her genuine feelings of repulsion. Amazingly, when he died, she had a complete change of heart. She actually felt affection for her late uncle. The therapist was satisfied with her, Paula was satisfied with herself: love had triumphed over her hatred and cured her of her allergies. Suddenly, however, she developed severe asthma and she was completely incapable of understanding this new illness. She had purged herself, she had forgiven her uncle and bore no malice against him. So why this punishment? She interpreted the outbreak of the illness as a retribution for her earlier feelings of anger and indignation. Then she read a book of mine, and her illness prompted her to write to me. Her asthma disappeared as soon as she relinquished her "love" for her uncle. It was an example of obedience, not love.

Another woman was astounded by the fact that after years of psychoanalysis she had pains in her legs that no doctor could find an explanation for. In the end, her physicians were forced to admit that the pains might be psychosomatic. In her analytic sessions she had been working for years on the so-called fantasy that she had been sexually abused by her father. More than anything else, she wanted to believe her analyst's version that these were fantasies and not real memories. But all these speculations did nothing to help her understand why she was in such pain. When she finally terminated the treatment, the pains in her legs vanished overnight! They had been a signal that she was living in a world that she could not "step out of." She wanted to run away from her analyst and his misguided—and misguiding—interpretations, but she did not dare to. For a time, the pains in her legs were able to block the need to escape, until she made the decision to terminate the analysis and no longer expect any benefit from it.

The attachment to parental figures I am trying to describe here is an attachment to parents who have inflicted injury on their children. It is an attachment that prevents us from helping ourselves. The unfulfilled natural needs of the child are later transferred to therapists, partners, or our own children. We cannot believe that those needs were really ignored, or possibly even trampled on by our parents in such a way that we were forced to repress them. We hope that the other people we relate to will finally give us what we have been looking for, understand, support, and respect us, and relieve us of the difficult decisions life brings with it. As these expectations are fostered by the denial of childhood reality, we cannot give them up. As I said earlier, they cannot be relinquished by an act of will. But they will disappear in time if we are determined to face up to our own truth. This is not easy. It is almost always painful. But it is possible.

In the forums, we frequently observe that some people get annoyed if others in the group respond to the deeds of their parents with indignation, although they do not know the parents and although their reaction is based entirely on the account given by the person in question. But it is one thing to complain about one's parents deeds and quite another to take the facts of the matter fully and completely seriously. The latter course arouses the infant's fear of punishment. Accordingly, many prefer to leave

their earliest perceptions in a state of repression, to avoid looking the truth in the face, to extenuate their parents' deeds, and to
reconcile themselves with the idea of forgiveness. But this attitude merely serves to perpetuate the futile expectations we have
entertained since our childhood.

I embarked on my first analysis in 1958. Looking back, I have
the impression that my analyst was strongly influenced by traditional morality. I was not aware of the fact myself because I had
grown up with the same system of values. Of course, this meant
that there was no chance for me to discover that I had been
abused as a child. To realize that fact I needed a witness who had
already made the same discovery herself, someone who no longer
shared the customary denial of child abuse that is prevalent in
our society. Today, over forty years later, this attitude is still anything but self-evident. Reports by therapists claiming to be on
the children's side normally betray a "corrective" attitude they are
completely unaware of because they have never reflected on the
fact. Although many such therapists quote from my books and
encourage their clients to do justice to themselves, rather than
adapt and adjust to the demands made on them by others, I
myself as a reader of their reports have the feeling that the advice
they mete out is in fact advice that cannot genuinely be followed.
What I describe as the result of a personal history is treated like
some kind of character flaw that needs to be corrected. We are
told to respect ourselves, to estimate our own qualities, and all
kinds of other things. There is a whole repertory of injunctions
designed to help people to regain their self-esteem. But the
barriers in their minds are resistant to these injunctions. As I see
it, the point is that people who cannot estimate and respect

themselves, who cannot allow themselves the free expression of their creativity, do not do so voluntarily. These barriers are the result of each person's individual story. They want to understand how they have become that way, then they need to know that story as precisely as possible and need to engage with it emotionally. Once they have understood this fact, and are actually able to feel the implications of the story (not just grasp them intellectually), then they will need no more advice. What these adults need then is an enlightened witness who can accompany them on the road to their own truth, help them embark on a process in the course of which they will finally permit themselves the always-wanted but always-denied things: trust, respect, and love for themselves. We must abandon the expectation that someday the parents will give us what they withheld in childhood.

This is the reason so few people have actually taken that road, why so many content themselves with the advice of their therapists or let religious notions prevent them from discovering their own truth. Earlier on, I suggested that fear is the decisive factor in all this. But I also believe that this fear will be reduced when the facts of childhood abuse are no longer treated as a taboo in our society. So far, the victims of such abuse have denied its existence because of the infant fear that lives on inside them. In this way they have contributed to the all-pervasive denial of the truth. But once the former victims begin to reveal what happened to them, then therapists too will be forced to acknowledge these realities. A short while ago, a well-known German psychoanalyst stated publicly that he rarely encountered former victims of childhood abuse in his practice. This is an astounding statement, because I know of literally no one who suffers from psychic symptoms and seeks treatment for them without having at least been beaten and humiliated in childhood. I call such treatment abuse, although for thousands of years it has been regarded as a legitimate parenting method. It may be no more than a question of definition, but in this case the definition is decisive.

9

The Carousel of Feelings

S OME TIME AGO, I happened to pass by a children's carousel and stopped for a moment to watch the little children enjoying themselves. By and large, the faces of the children, most of whom were about two years old, did indeed reflect feelings of pleasure and exhilaration. But in some of them it was also possible to discern the fear they felt at being whirled around at such speed with no one on board to protect them. That fear was mixed with pride at being "big" enough to sit at the steering wheel of their little car, to be in the driving seat. Other feelings were probably involved too: curiosity about what might happen next, and concern to keep visual contact with their parents. I could see how all these feelings asserted themselves at different times, and I observed how they found expression in response to the thrill of such unexpected motion.

When I left the playground, I found myself wondering what

exactly takes place in the mind of a little two-year-old child when its body is used to gratify the sexual needs of adults. What can have prompted such a thought? Perhaps I had identified a tension, a species of distrust mixed in with the enjoyment these children were displaying. Going round and round at such speed may have appeared to their bodies as something alien, unaccustomed, frightening. When they finally got off the carousel, their faces were anxious, confused; all of them held on tightly to their parents. It occurred to me that perhaps this kind of pleasure is not natural at that age, not something that is truly and genuinely attuned to the minds or spirits of such small children. It is a source of artificial enjoyment that the carousel operator makes money from. It was this thought that prompted me to ask myself what a little girl feels like when she has been sexually abused? What is it like if her mother hardly touches her because she rejects her own daughter and conceals all her affectionate feelings from herself because of what happened to her in her own childhood? Then the girl will be so starved of affection that she will respond to almost any kind of physical contact with gratitude as the fulfillment of an urgent desire. But indistinctly the child will sense that her true nature, her longing for genuine communication and physical affection, is in fact merely being exploited by the father, if her body is used exclusively as a stimulus for masturbation or as a means of asserting adult power.

It may be that this little girl will suppress her feelings of disappointment, grief, and rage at the betrayal of her true self, at the unfulfilled promise. Maybe she will continue to cling to the father because she cannot abandon the hope that one day he will redeem the promise implicit in those first caresses, and restore the child's dignity and show her what love really is. For there is no one else in her whole environment who has made her such a promise of love. But this hope can be destructive.

It may well be that in adulthood this girl will suffer from a compulsion to mutilate herself and be forced to seek therapy because she can achieve a feeling of pleasure only by hurting herself. In fact, hurting herself is the only way in which she can feel anything at all, because the abuse at the hands of her father has led to a situation where she has killed off her own feelings almost entirely and thus no longer has them at her disposal. Alternatively, a woman who has been through this kind of nightmare may suffer from genital eczema, as described by the German author Kristina Meyer in her 1994 book *The Double Secret* (not available in English). When she turned to a psychoanalyst for help, she displayed a whole range of symptoms that indicated very clearly that she must have been sexually abused by her father in infancy. Her analyst did not immediately suspect this, but she did at least accompany Kristina very conscientiously to a point where Kristina herself was able to unearth the story of the cruel, brutal violations she had suffered at the hands of her father from the repression to which she had consigned it. The process lasted six years in a rigorous analytic setting, later followed by group therapy and body therapy.

This process could probably have been shortened if the analyst had been able to allow herself from the outset to recognize the genital eczema as an indication of early exploitation of the child's body. Sixteen years ago, this was obviously not yet possible. Questioned by Kristina about her attitude, the analyst said that Kristina would not have been able to live with that knowledge before a good working analytic relationship had been established.

At the time I might have believed the same thing. But on the basis of my later experiences I tend to believe that it can never be too early to tell a formerly abused child what one has clearly recognized and to offer to side with that person unreservedly. Kristina Meyer struggled with unbelievable courage to find out and face up to her own truth, and she deserved from the outset to be guided out of the darkness she was trapped in. She dreamed repeatedly of the moment when her analyst would take her in her arms and console her. But her analyst remained faithful to her tenets and never fulfilled Kristina's harmless wish. If she had done so, she might have been able to convey to Kristina an important message: There are loving embraces that, while they fully respect the boundaries of the other person, alleviate the feeling of being alone in the world. Today, at a time when all kinds of body therapies are available, this obstinate refusal to fulfill such a desire by an analyst who was otherwise fully and excruciatingly sensible to the tragedy of her patient may appear strange. From a psychoanalytic vantage, however, it is understandable, and it is only respecting the rules.

At this point I would like to return to the image of the carousel I referred to at the beginning of this chapter. We will recall that in my eyes the faces of the little children riding on the carousel betrayed not only pleasure but also fear and disquiet. My comparison with an incest situation makes no claim to universality. It was an idea that suddenly occurred to me. Yet the fact that, as children and adults, we are frequently exposed to contradictory emotions demands to be taken seriously. If, as small children, we have to deal with adults who have never tried to clarify their own feelings, this can expose us to a species of chaos that is unsettling in the extreme. To escape from these feelings of confusion and uncertainty, we activate the mechanism of repression and disassociation. We feel no fear, we love our parents, we trust them, and we try to live up to their expectations, so that they can be pleased with us. Only later, in adulthood, does this fear reassert itself, frequently in connection with the partners we have chosen. We find it impossible to understand. Here, as in childhood, we want nothing more than to accept the other's contradictions without a word, because we want to be loved. But the body asserts its claim to the truth and will produce symptoms if we go on denying or ignoring the rage, the fear, the indignation, and the horror of a child that has been sexually abused.

The trouble is that, however hard we try, we will never be able to locate those childhood situations if we neglect the engagement with them in the present. Only in the liberation from present dependency can we repair the harm that has been done, and this means identifying and resolving the consequences of that early dependency. Here is an example. Andreas, a middle-aged incest survivor, had been suffering from overweight for a number of years and suspected that this distressing symptom had something to do with his relationship with his authoritarian father, who was cruel to him in his childhood. But he could not master the situation. He did everything he could to reduce weight and followed all his doctor's instructions; he could even feel his anger at the father's behavior in his childhood. But none of this helped. Andreas had occasional outbreaks of rage: he scolded his children, although he had no desire to do so, and bawled at his partner, although he had no desire to do that either. He resorted to alcohol to calm down, but did not consider himself an alcoholic. He wanted to be kind to his family, and the wine helped him tame his violent rage and experience pleasant feelings.

In one of our interviews, Andreas mentioned in passing that

he was unable to dissuade his parents from dropping in whenever it suited them; they never phoned him beforehand to tell him of their intentions. I asked whether he had requested they desist from this habit. He responded with alacrity, saying that he had repeatedly asked them to give him some warning beforehand, but they took no notice. The parents felt that they were entitled to look in whenever they like because the house belonged to them. Surprised, I asked him why they called his house their own property. Andreas told me that he was indeed the tenant of a house that belonged to his parents and paid them rent. I asked him whether there might be another house that he could rent for the same, or possibly a slightly higher sum. This, after all, would make him independent of his parents and prevent them from dropping in whenever it occurred to them and trespassing on his time. His eyes widened. He said that he had never thought about this possibility before.

This may seem surprising. But it becomes less so if one bears in mind that this man was still entrapped in the childlike situation in which he had to yield to the will, the power, and the authority of his engulfing parents, and where he was unable to see any way out of it for fear of being rejected by them. This fear still dogged him; he still ate far too much, even when he did his best to stick to a diet. But his need for the right "nourishment"— that is, his need to be independent of his parents and to ensure his own well-being—was so strong that it could only be gratified in an appropriate way, not by eating too much. Food can never satisfy this hunger for freedom. The freedom to eat and drink as much as one likes cannot appease the hunger for self-determination. It cannot be a substitute for genuine freedom.

As Andreas was leaving, he said with an air of determination,

"I'm going to put an ad in the paper right away and look for a place of my own. And I'll find one, believe me!" Only a few days later, Andreas told me he had found a house he liked better than the one that belonged to his parents and that was also cheaper to rent. Why did it take so long for him to hit on this simple solution? Because as long as he was in his parents' house, Andreas still hoped his mother and father might give him what he had longed for as a child. But what they denied him as a child could not be made up for when he grew up. They still treated him like their own property, never listened to him when he expressed his wishes, considered it quite natural that he should renovate the house and invest money in it without any kind of recompense, because they were his parents and as such simply assumed that they had a right to expect it. Only in his exchanges with the enlightened witness I represented for him did he suddenly realize the situation he was in. Only then did he become aware that he was letting himself be exploited, just like when he was a child and believed that he ought to be grateful into the bargain. Now he could give up the illusion that his parents might change some day.

A few months later he wrote to me:

My parents tried to make me feel guilty when I terminated the rental agreement. They didn't want to let me go. When they realized they could no longer force me to do something against my own will, they offered to reduce the rent and pay back some of the money I had invested. I realized then that it was not I who had profited from this contract but them. I refused all their proposals.

The whole process, however, was anything but painless. I

had to look the truth in the eye, and the truth hurt. I felt the suffering of the little child I once was, a child who was never loved, never listened to, never taken any notice of, a child who let himself be exploited, hoping that someday things might be different. The miracle was that the more I felt, the more weight I lost. I didn't need strong drink to numb my feelings, I started seeing things straight again, and if I had an occasional fit of rage I knew who the real targets were: not my children, not my wife, but my mother and father, from whom I could now withdraw my love. I realized that this love was only the desire to be loved, a desire that was never fulfilled. I had to get rid of that desire. Suddenly I didn't need to eat as much as I used to, I was less tired, I had all my energy at my command, which had a bearing on my work as well.

In time, my anger at my parents also cooled off, because now if I need something I do it myself, instead of waiting for them to do it. I no longer force myself to love them (why should I?), and I no longer fear that I will feel guilty when they are dead, as my sister has prophesied. I think that their death will be a relief, because then the constraint to be insincere and hypocritical will disappear. But I am already trying to free myself of that constraint. My parents asked my sister to tell me that my letters had become very down-to-earth and factual. They found this hurtful because they felt I was not so affectionate as I used to be. They wanted me back the way I was. I can't do it, and I don't want to do it either. I no longer intend to play the role they have allotted to me in their little drama. After a long search, I found a therapist who made a good impression on me, someone I can talk to the way I used to talk to you, frankly, without sparing my parents, without covering up the truth, my own truth. And above all, I'm glad I was able to make the decision to leave the house that bound me for so long to hopes that could never be fulfilled.

I once initiated a discussion on the Fourth Commandment by asking what the love of one's parents consisted of exactly, even if they were cruel to us in our childhood. The answers came quickly, with little time for reflection. Various feelings were named: compassion for the old people, who were frequently also ill or frail; gratitude for the gift of life and the good days when one was not beaten; fear of being an evil person; the conviction that we must forgive our parents' deeds because otherwise we will never be truly adult. This triggered a heated discussion, in which these views were challenged. One participant, Ruth, said with unexpected vehemence:

My life is proof positive that the Fourth Commandment is wrong. Once I freed myself from the claims made on me by my parents and stopped living up to their expectations, overt or covert, I started feeling healthier than I had ever felt before. I lost all my symptoms, I stopped being irritable with my children, and I now believe that all those things had happened because I was trying to comply with a commandment that did not do my body any good.

Ruth thought this commandment had such power over us because it supports the anxiety and the feelings of guilt our parents have inculcated into us at a very early age. She herself had been a prey to enormous anxiety shortly before she realized that she did not love her parents. She had only *wanted* to love them and accordingly pretended both to herself and them that she actually did. Once she became aware of this, the anxiety disappeared.

I think many people might feel the same way if they had someone say to them, "You don't need to love and honor your parents. They did you harm. You don't need to force yourself to feel things you don't really feel. Constraint and enforcement have never produced anything good. In your case they can be destructive; your body will pay the price."

This discussion confirmed my impression that we sometimes spend all our lives obeying a phantom that goes by the name of upbringing, morality, or religion. It forces us to ignore, repress, or fight against our natural, biological needs, and finally we pay for this with illnesses that we neither understand nor want to understand and that we try to overcome with medication. When patients undergoing therapy actually manage to achieve access to their true selves through the awakening of their repressed emotions, some therapists, inspired no doubt by Alcoholics Anonymous, attribute this to the agency of a "higher power." By doing so, they undermine the trust we all have in ourselves from the outset: the trust in our ability to sense what will do us good and what will not.

In my case, my father and mother systematically drove this trust out of me from birth. I had to learn to see and judge everything I felt through my mother's eyes and to systematically kill off my real feelings and needs. Accordingly, in the course of time I was seriously handicapped in my ability to feel my own needs and to go in search of their gratification. For example, it took me forty-eight years to discover the need to paint and to allow myself to gratify that need. Finally, that need asserted itself. It took me even longer to concede myself the right not to love my parents.

In the course of time, I realized more and more clearly how the effort of loving someone who had almost ruined my life was doing me serious harm. It was estranging me from my own truth, forcing me to deceive myself, constraining me to adopt a role my parents foisted on to me so early—the role of the "good girl" forced to comply with emotional demands masquerading as upbringing and morality. As I gradually learned to be true to myself and succeeded in admitting my own feelings, the language of my body spoke out more and more clearly and guided me toward decisions that did it good and helped it to express its natural needs. I was able to stop joining in other people's games, to stop telling myself that my parents had their good sides, to stop confusing myself over and over again as I did when I was a child. I was able to decide in favor of adulthood. And the confusion disappeared.

I know now that my parents did not want me. Their parents forced the marriage on them. I was the unloved product of two well-behaved children who owed their parents a debt of obedience and brought a child into the world whom they did not want. They were hoping for a little boy, because that was what the two grandfathers wanted. But they got a little girl instead, and for decades that girl did all she could to compensate them for the happiness they had missed out on. This undertaking was doomed to failure. However, as a child intent on surviving, I had no choice but to do the best I could. From the outset I received the implicit injunction from my parents to give them the acknowledgment, attention, and love that their own parents had withheld from them. If that attempt was to succeed, I had to give up my own truth, the truth of my own feelings. Despite these efforts I was long dogged by profound feelings of guilt, for this was an injunction that I could not comply with. In addition, I denied myself something of paramount importance: my own truth. (This was something I began to suspect when I wrote *The Drama of the Gifted Child*, a book in which so many readers identified their own fates.) Yet, for decades to come, I went on trying to fulfill this mission, even when I reached adulthood. I tried it with my partners, with my friends, with my children. Every time I attempted to extricate myself from the duty of rescuing others from their confusion, the feeling of guilt almost killed me. Only very late in life did I finally succeed.

Sloughing off gratitude and guilt feelings was an extremely important stage on the path to breaking with my dependency on my internalized parents. But there were other steps that had to be taken as well. The most important of these was giving up the expectation and the hope that what I missed most sorely in my relations with my parents—a frank exchange of feelings, the freedom to communicate—might someday be possible after all. It did indeed become possible, with other people, but only after I had realized the whole truth about my childhood. Then I understood how impossible it was to communicate freely with my parents and how much suffering that had caused me as a child. My parents have been dead for a long time now, but I can imagine that for people whose parents are still alive this process is even more arduous. The expectations originating in childhood can be so strong that we will give up everything that would do us good, in order finally to be the way our parents wanted us to be and thus sustain the illusion of love.

Karl, for example, describes his confusion as follows:

> I love my mother, but she doesn't believe me, because she confuses me with my father, who made life hell for her. But I

am not like my father. She makes me livid, but I don't want to show my anger, because then she would have the proof that I am like my father after all. And that's not true. So I have to curb my anger, so as not to prove her right, and then I don't feel love for her, only hate. I don't want that hate, I want to be seen and loved by her the way I am, not hated like my father. What's the right thing for me to do?

The answer is that we can never do the right thing as long as we are out to please someone else. We can only be the people we are, and we cannot force our parents to love us. There are parents who can love only the mask their child wears. When the child removes that mask, they frequently say, as we saw earlier with Andreas, "All I want is for you to be the way you were before."

The illusion that we can still "earn" our parents' love can be upheld only by denying what actually happened. That illusion crumples as soon as we have taken the decision to look the truth in the face, with all its ramifications, and to abandon the self-deception we have cultivated with the aid of alcohol, drugs, and medication. Anna, a thirty-five-year-old mother of two, asked me, "What can I say to my mother when she keeps on telling me that all she wants is for me to show her my love? 'You used to do that,' she says, 'and now you're so different.' I'd like to say, 'Yes, because now I feel that I wasn't always sincere to you. I want to be truthful.' "

"And why can't you say just that?" I asked.

"That's true," said Anna. "I have the right to stick up for my own truth. And basically she has the right to hear from me that what she feels is true. That's very simple in theory, but compassion has prevented me from being frank with my mother. I was sorry for her. She was never loved as a child; she was given away at birth. She clung to my love, and I didn't want to take it away from her."

"Are you her only child?" I asked.

"No, she has five children, and they all do what they can to be of service to her. But that obviously doesn't fill the gap that she has been carrying around inside her since her childhood."

"So you think you can fill that gap by telling her a lie?"

"No, not that. You're right. Why do I want to give her the love I don't feel, just for compassion's sake? I always had all kinds of illnesses. Now they've gone away. They went away as soon as I admitted to myself that I have never really loved my mother because I felt engulfed and emotionally blackmailed by her. But actually telling her that made me afraid, and now I ask myself what I thought this compassion would do for her. It's nothing but a lie. I owe it to my own body not to perpetuate it any longer."

So what is left of "love" when we take a closer look at the real emotions behind it, as I have tried to do here? Gratitude, compassion, illusion, denial of the truth, guilt feelings, deceit—these are all ingredients of an attachment that frequently makes us ill and cannot do our parents any real good. Everywhere in the world, this pathological attachment is regarded as love. Whenever I express this idea, I come up against all kinds of anxiety and resistance. But when, in the course of discussion, I succeed in explaining what I mean, that resistance melts away very quickly, and many people respond with a kind of illumination that surprises them.

A person once said, "It's true. Why do I think it would kill my parents if I showed them what I really felt for them? I have the right to feel what I feel. It's not a question of retaliation, but of honesty. Why is honesty upheld as an abstract concept in religious instruction at school but prohibited in the relationship with our parents?"

Indeed, how wonderful it would be if we could talk honestly to our parents. What they ultimately make of the things we say to them is something we have no influence on. But it would be an opportunity for us, for our children, and not least for our body, which has after all shown us the way to the truth.

This ability of the body is a source of never-ending wonder to me. It fights against lies with a tenacity and a shrewdness that are properly astounding. Moral and religious claims cannot deceive or confuse it. A little child is force-fed morality. He accepts this nourishment willingly because he loves his parents, and suffers countless illnesses in his school years. As an adult he makes use of his superb intellect to fight against conventional morality, possibly becoming a philosopher or a writer in the process. But his true feelings about his family, which were masked by illness during his school days, have a stunting effect on him, as was the case with Nietzsche and Schiller. Finally, he becomes a victim of his parents, sacrificing himself to their ideas of morality and religion, even though as an adult he saw so clearly through the lies of "society." Seeing through his own self-deception, realizing that he had let himself be made the sacrifice of morality, was more difficult for him than penning philosophical tracts or writing courageous dramas. But it is only the internal processes taking place in the individual, not the thoughts divorced from our own bodies, that can bring about a productive change in our mentality.

Those lucky enough to experience love and understanding in childhood will have no problems with the truth. They have been able to develop their abilities to the full, and the children will profit from that. I have no idea how large the percentage of such people actually is. I do know that beatings are still recommended as a method of parenting; that the United States, that self-styled model of democracy, still allows corporal punishment in schools in twenty-two states; and that, if anything, these states are becoming more and more vocal in their defense of this "right" to which all parents are entitled. It is absurd to believe that we can teach children democracy with the help of physical force.

My conclusion from this is that there are probably a lot of people living in the world right now who have been through this kind of upbringing. All of them had their resistance to cruelty clubbed down at a very early stage; all of them have grown up in a state of what I can only call "inner insincerity." We can observe this wherever we look. If someone says, "I don't love my parents because they constantly humiliated me," she will immediately hear the same advice from all sides: She must change her attitude if she wants to become truly adult, she must not live with hatred bottled up inside herself if she wants to stay healthy; she can free herself of that hatred only if she forgives her parents; there is no such thing as ideal parents—all parents sometimes make mistakes, and this is something we have to put up with, and we can learn to do so once we are truly adult.

The reason such advice sounds so sensible is that we have heard it all our lives and have believed it to be sound. But it is not. It rests on fallacious assumptions. It is not true that forgiveness will free us from hatred. It merely helps to cover it up and hence to reinforce it (in our unconscious minds). It is not true that tolerance grows with age. On the contrary. Children will tolerate their parents' absurdities because they think them normal and have no way of defending themselves against them. Not until adulthood do we actively suffer from this lack of freedom and these constraints. But we feel this suffering in our relations with others, with our partners and our children. Infant fear of our parents stops us from recognizing the truth. It is not true that hatred makes us ill. Repressed, disassociated emotions can make us ill but not conscious feelings that we can give expression to.[1] As adults, we will hate only if we remain trapped in a situation in which we cannot give free expression to our feelings. It is this dependency that makes us start to hate. As soon as we break that dependency (which as adults we can normally do, unless we are prisoners of some totalitarian regime), as soon as we free ourselves from that slavery, then we will no longer hate (see Chapter 10). However, if hatred is there it is no good forbidding it, as all the religions do. We have to understand the reasons for it if we are to opt for the kind of behavior that will free people from the dependency that breeds hatred.

Of course, people who have been severed from their true feelings since early childhood will be dependent on institutions like the church and will let themselves be told what they are allowed to feel. In most cases it is very little indeed. But I cannot imagine that it will always be like this. Somewhere, sometime, there will be a rebellion, and the process of mutual stultification will be halted. It will be halted when individuals summon up the courage to overcome their understandable fears, to tell, feel, and publish the truth and communicate with others on this basis.

Once we realize the immense amount of energy children can summon up in order to survive cruelty and extreme sadism, things suddenly start looking more optimistic. Then it is easy to imagine that our world could be a much better one if those children (like Rimbaud, Schiller, Dostoevsky, and Nietzsche) could expend their almost limitless energies on other, more productive ends than merely fighting for their own survival.

10

The Body as Guardian
of the Truth

THE STORY OF ELIZABETH, age twenty-eight, provides a clear example of how painful and, ultimately, how successful separation from a parent can be. She writes:

My mother was extremely cruel to me when I was small. She would punch me on the head, throw me against the wall, and pull my hair if things didn't suit her. I had no way of preventing this because I could never understand the real cause of such outbreaks and thus avoid them the next time round. So I did my very best to detect the slightest changes of mood in my mother from the outset, hoping I could avoid her fits of rage by adapting to them in some way. I was sometimes successful, but most of the time I wasn't.

A few years back I started suffering from depression. I went to see a therapist and told her a lot of things about my childhood. At first things went very well indeed. She looked like she was listening to me, and that made everything a great deal easier. Sometimes she did say things I didn't like too much. But, as always, I managed to ignore my own feelings and adjust to her mentality. She appeared to be much influenced by oriental philosophy. At first I thought this needn't bother me as long as she was prepared to listen to what I had to say. Then my therapist started trying to persuade me that I must make peace with my mother if I didn't want to spend my whole life consumed by hatred. Then I really lost my temper and terminated the therapy. I told my therapist that as far as my feelings for my mother were concerned, I was better informed than she was.

All I had to do was to listen to my own body, because in all the encounters with my mother I was invariably afflicted with severe physical symptoms as soon as I started repressing my feelings. My body appears to be completely unerring in this respect, and my impression is that it knows my truth very well; better than my conscious self, it knows all about what I went through with my mother. It does not allow me to distort myself to comply with conventional regulations or precepts. As long as I take its messages seriously and act in accordance with them, I no longer suffer from migraine and lumbago, and I do not feel isolated. I have found people I can talk to about my childhood, people who understand me because they have similar memories, and I do not intend to consult any more therapists. It would be nice if I could find someone who would let me be as I am, let me say all the things I would like to say, who would not force-feed me with moralistic homilies. This might help me integrate my painful memories. But I'm on the way to doing that as it is, with the help of some of my friends. I am closer to my own feelings than I have ever been before. I can express them in two self-help groups and try out a new form of communication in which I feel at ease. Since I started doing that, my physical complaints and my depression have more or less disappeared.

This sounded very encouraging, so it came as no surprise to me, one year later, when Elizabeth wrote once again to tell me the following:

I have not had any more therapy, and I'm doing fine. I haven't seen my mother once this year, and I do not feel the need to do so. The memories of her cruelty to me when I was small are so vivid that they protect me from any illusions I might have and also from expectations that she might have something to give me that I missed out on so much as a child. Even though I still miss it from time to time, I now know exactly where there is absolutely no point in looking for it. In contrast to what my therapist prophesied, I feel no hatred in me. I do not need to hate my mother because I am no longer emotionally dependent on her.

My therapist failed to understand that. She wanted to free me of my hatred and did not realize that she was unintentionally thrusting me into that hate, which was an expression of my dependency, a dependency she would have created all over again. If I had followed my therapist's advice, that hatred would have reared its head once more. Today, I no longer need to suffer from pretending that I have feelings for my mother. I don't. That is why there is no hatred left inside me. It was always the hatred of a dependent child, and I would have perpetuated it with my therapist if I had not left her in time.

I was very happy about the solution Elizabeth had found. But what about people who do not have such perspicacity and strength? Such people really do need a therapist who can support them in their quest for themselves without making moral claims on them. Reading accounts of successful and unsuccessful therapies may perhaps heighten the therapists' awareness, so that they can free themselves of the venom of poisonous pedagogy and not continue to spread it in their work.

It does not matter so much whether we have to break off all contact with our parents or not. The process of separation, the path from childhood to adulthood, takes place *inside* us. Sometimes breaking off all contact is the only way in which we can live up to our own needs. And if contact does appear to make sense, it should be only when we are clear in our minds about what we can take and what we cannot, only after we not only know what happened to us but can also assess *what it did to us*, what effect it had on us. Every individual life story is different, and the external form that relationships take can display an infinite range of variations. But there are three common factors:

1. The old wounds can heal over only when survivors of maltreatment have made a decision in favor of change, when they have decided to respect themselves and can liberate themselves from the expectations of the child within.
2. Parents do not change automatically as a result of the understanding and forgiveness bestowed upon them by their children. They alone can institute such change, if they really want to.
3. As long as the pain born of those injuries is denied, there will be someone paying the price in terms of sanity and health— either the former victim or his/her children.

Children who have been badly treated and have thus never been able to grow up will try all their lives to do justice to the "good sides" of their tormentors and will pin all hopes and expectations to that attempt. This, for example, was the attitude first adopted by Elizabeth: "Sometimes my mother would read me a story, and that was nice. Sometimes she took me into her confidence and told me about her worries. Then I felt like someone elect. She would never beat me on occasions like that, so I felt like I was out of danger." Reports like this remind me of Imre Kertész's description of his arrival in Auschwitz. He invariably looked on the bright side, so as to fend off the fear he instinctively felt and thus survive. But Auschwitz was unalterably Auschwitz in all its horrors. It was only decades later that he was able to gauge and actually feel what this cripplingly humiliating system had done to his inner self.

I would not like this reference to Kertész and his death-camp experiences to be taken to mean that one should not forgive one's parents if they realize what they have done and apologize. This kind of thing can happen, once parents start daring to feel and can accordingly understand the pain they inflicted on their child. But it is rare. What frequently does occur is a continuation of the dependency relationship, this time the other way round. The frail and ailing parents seek support from their adult children and use the effective instrument of accusation to obtain compassion. This compassion may be the very thing that has impeded the child's development—a development toward adulthood. Unwanted children will always have been afraid of their own need for life.

The perception stored away in the body of an unwanted child is a repressed perception, but it is nonetheless accurate for that:

"They want to kill me. I'm in mortal danger." This perception can vanish from the adult mind once it has become conscious. Then the former emotion (fear, anxiety, stress) will turn into a memory that says: "I *was* in danger before but I am not any longer." Normally, such a conscious memory is either preceded or accompanied by the experience of the old emotions and by feelings of grief.

Once we have learned to live with our feelings and not to fight against them, we see in the manifestations of our bodies not a danger but helpful indications about our own personal history.

11

Can I Say It?

I CAN WELL REMEMBER the fears that haunted me when I was writing *Thou Shalt Not Be Aware*. At the time I was much preoccupied with the fact that for three hundred years the Roman Catholic Church was able to deny successfully the truth of Galileo Galilei's discoveries and that his body responded by inflicting blindness on him when he was forced to contradict what he had found out. A feeling of helplessness descended on me. I knew quite definitely that I had chanced on an unwritten law, the devastating exploitation of children for the retaliatory needs of their parents and the taboo placed on that reality by society. We shall not be aware.

Did I not risk incurring the severest of penalties if I insisted on breaking that taboo? But my fear also helped me to understand a lot of things, one of them being that Freud betrayed his own insights for that very reason. Should I follow in his footsteps and revoke the insights I had gained on the frequency and the consequences of cruelty to children, so as not to be attacked and rejected? Could I really have seen something that so many people who unconditionally adulated Freud had not seen: his self-deception? I can remember that whenever I started negotiating with myself, trying to find a compromise, or asking myself whether I should not perhaps divulge only part of the truth, physical symptoms were invariably the response. I had digestive problems, I could not sleep, and I suffered from bouts of depression. Once I had realized that there were no more compromises for me, those symptoms disappeared.

The response to the publication was indeed one of total rejection, both of me and my book by the scientific world, a world in which I still felt "at home" at the time. This rejection remains. But I am no longer a child, and my life no longer depends on recognition from "the family." The book has found its own path. Today the "forbidden" statements in it are more or less taken for granted, both by laypeople and experts. Many people have since concurred with my criticism of Freud, and the severe consequences of cruelty to children are now being given more attention by the experts as well. I have not been killed, and I have heard my voice assert itself. From this experience I derive the trust that *The Body Never Lies* too will be understood. Initially, it may come as a shock to some people. But many who wish to understand themselves will understand this book. The shock effect will also wear off as soon as people realize that they are not alone with their knowledge and—above all—that they are no longer exposed to the dangers of their childhood.

JUDITH'S SITUATION, which I will relay here, once again underscores the need for the right therapist. As a child, Judith, now forty, was sexually abused by her father in the most brutal way imaginable. Her mother never protected her. In therapy Judith succeeded in reversing the repression and curing the symptoms, once she had achieved separation from her parents. But the fear of punishment, which she had kept disassociated up to the start of therapy and learned to feel only through that therapy, remained with her for a long time. This was largely due to her therapist's opinion that it would be impossible to regain health and full sanity as long as she cut herself off completely from her parents. Accordingly, Judith made an attempt to approach her mother and talk things over with her. On every occasion, the response was total rejection and condemnation. Her mother told her, "There are things that one must never say to one's parents on any account." Accusation and criticism flew in the face of the Fourth Commandment and were accordingly an insult to God.

Her mother's responses helped Judith to see the limitations of her therapist, who herself was the prisoner of a schematic view that gave her the fallacious conviction that she knew all about the things that one may, must, or must not do. With the help of another therapist, Judith realized how grateful her body was to her for no longer forcing herself into relationships like these. As a child she had not had this choice. She was forced to live with a mother who had looked on indifferently as she suffered and who responded with platitudes to everything Judith told her. Whenever Judith said anything out of line with those platitudes, anything truly and wholly her own, she was penalized with total rejection. Such rejection has the same effect on the child as the loss of the mother and is thus equivalent to a situation of mortal danger. Fear of this danger could not be allayed in the first course of therapy because the moral claims made on Judith by her therapist constantly gave that feeling new nourishment.

The influences I am talking about here are usually very subtle, subtle enough to be all but imperceptible. The reason for this is that they harmonize more or less completely with the traditional values we have all grown up with. It was long taken for granted— and still is today—that the Fourth Commandment has to be obeyed, that all parents have the right to be honored even if they behaved destructively toward their children. But as soon as we have opted out of this value system we will consider it entirely absurd for an adult woman to be expected to honor her parents either for being brutally cruel to her, or for looking on and failing to intervene.

Yet this absurdity is generally considered normal. It is astonishing to find even renowned therapists and authors unable to extricate themselves from the conviction that forgiving one's parents is the crowning glory of a successful course of therapy. Though today this conviction is upheld with less certainty than was the case only a few years ago, the expectations bound up with it are unmistakable and contain the message Heaven help you if you disregard the Fourth Commandment! While these authors frequently say that there should be no hurry, that forgiveness should not take place at the beginning of therapy because the strong emotions involved first need to be admitted to, they also insist that one day the patient must be mature enough to forgive. On this point there appears to be general agreement. These experts take it for granted that the goal of the therapy is being able to wholeheartedly forgive one's parents. I believe this opinion to be misguided. The goal of a successful therapy is liberation from a painful dependency—not reconciliation, which is only a moralistic and not a physiological demand. The body does not consist solely of the heart, and our brain is not just some receptacle into which these absurdities and contradictions have been poured during religious instruction classes. It is an organism that retains the complete memory of everything that has happened to it. Anyone genuinely alive to this insight would say, "God cannot expect me to believe something that in my eyes is contradictory and does vital harm to me."

Can we expect therapists to set themselves up against the value systems of our parents in order to help us to find our own truth, if this is necessary? I believe that we can and must expect this when we embark on a course of therapy, especially if we have reached a stage where we can start taking the messages of our bodies seriously. Dagmar, a young woman, writes:

My mother has heart disease. I would like to be nice to her and talk to her at her bedside. I try to go and see her as often as I can. But every time I go, I get these intolerable headaches. I wake up in the night, bathed in sweat, and finally end up in a mood of depression with thoughts of suicide. In my dreams I see myself as the child she used to drag across the floor, crying, crying, crying. How can I get all that together? I have to go and see her because she's my mother. But I don't want to kill myself, and I don't want to be ill. I need someone to help me, to tell me how I can find peace of mind. I don't want to lie to myself, and I don't want to lie to my mother by playing her dear little daughter. But I don't want to be heartless and leave her all on her own with her illness.

A few years ago, Dagmar completed a course of therapy in which she forgave her mother for the cruelties she had inflicted on her. But in the face of her mother's severe illness, the old emotions she felt when she was a child caught up with her, and she had no idea of how to deal with them. She would rather take her own life than fail to live up to the expectations of her mother, of society, of her therapists. She would like nothing more than to visit her mother as a loving daughter, but she could not do so without deceiving herself. Her body told her that in no uncertain terms.

This example is not designed to suggest that one should on no account be a loving child to one's parents when they are near death. This is something that everyone will have to decide for themselves. But if our bodies remind us so sternly of the cruelties we once suffered, then we have no choice. We must listen seriously to what our bodies are telling us. Sometimes, complete strangers may be better companions for parents facing death because they have not suffered at their hands. They have no need to force themselves to tell lies, they have no need to pay for what they do with depression, and they can show their compassion without having to pretend. But a son or daughter may struggle in vain to summon up feelings of kindness and empathy, feelings that may stubbornly refuse to come. The reason for this is that the adult children are still attached to their parents with all the expectations they have vainly sustained throughout the years. When their parents lie dying, they desperately hope to feel, at the very last moment, the acceptance and confirmation that they never felt in the presence of their parents throughout their whole lives. Dagmar writes:

Every time I talk to my mother I feel a poison flowing into my body and forming an ulcer there. I try not to see it like that, because seeing it like that gives me guilt feelings. Then the ulcer starts to suppurate, and every time I lapse into depression. I try to admit my true feelings and tell myself I have the right to feel them, to see the intensity of my anger. When I admit my feelings, although they are not always good feelings, I start to breathe again. I start allowing myself to stay with my true feelings. If I succeed in that, I feel better, more alive, and my depression disappears.

And yet I seemingly cannot give up trying to understand my mother, to accept her as she is, to forgive her for everything she has done. I pay for it every time with depression. I don't know whether this realization is sufficient to heal the wounds, but I take my experiences very seriously—unlike my first therapist, who kept on trying to help me improve the relationship with my mother. She could not accept it the way it was. Neither could I. But how can I respect myself if I don't take my true feelings seriously? If I don't do that, I don't know who I am, I don't know who I'm supposed to be respecting.

This desire to be different from the way we are so as to make life easier for our parents in old age and perhaps finally receive love from them is understandable. But it is in direct opposition to the genuine need, supported by the body, to be true to our own selves. I believe that self-respect will come of its own accord once this need can be gratified.

12

Kill Rather Than Feel the Truth

NTIL RECENTLY, the phenomenon of serial killers
was mainly discussed by psychiatric experts. These
authorities took very little note of the childhood of
delinquents and essentially regarded criminals as people who
were born with depraved instincts. In the last few decades,
things appear to be changing for the better, and there is a more
genuine concern to understand. A 2003 article in the French
newspaper *Le Monde*[1] went into astonishing detail about the
childhood of Patrice Alègre, who murdered five women and
raped a sixth between 1990 and 1997, and the facts referred to
there make it absolutely clear why this man committed the
crimes that landed him in prison for life. To understand how
such dreadful murders come about, we require neither complicated psychological theories nor the simpleminded assumption
that some people are just born evil. What we need is insight into

the family atmosphere the child grew up in. But such insight is rare, because the criminal's parents are almost invariably treated with indulgence and exonerated from blame.

The article in Le Monde took a different view. In the space of a few paragraphs it presented the outline of a childhood that leaves not the slightest doubt about the reasons behind this criminal career. Patrice Alègre was the eldest child of a very young couple who did not want any children. His father was a policeman, and during the proceedings Patrice told the court that, as soon as he came home, he would start beating and berating his son. Patrice hated his father and sought refuge with his mother, who allegedly loved him and whom he served unswervingly. She was a prostitute, and she used the child as a lookout when she was entertaining her customers. Patrice had to stand at the door and give the alarm whenever some danger was in the offing (presumably the return of his angry father). Patrice said that, while he did not always have to watch what was going on in the next room, he was unable to stop up his ears and suffered immeasurably from his mother's constant moaning and whimpering. As a little child he had observed her engaging in oral sex, a sight that caused him panic and fear.

There may be many children who survive a confusing fate without turning criminal at a later date. Children frequently have almost inexhaustible reserves to draw upon in this respect. Such a child may even achieve fame, like Edgar Allan Poe, who ultimately drank himself to death, or Guy de Maupassant, who "came to terms" with his confused and tragic childhood by engaging with it in no fewer than 300 short stories. But he too, like his younger brother before him, became a psychotic and died in an asylum at the age of forty-two.

Patrice Alègre did not have the good fortune to find one single person who might have saved him from the hell he was trapped in and enabled him to see the crimes of his parents for what they were. Accordingly, he came to believe that his immediate environment was the world itself. He did everything to assert himself in that world and to escape his parents' omnipotence by means of theft, drugs, and violence. He told the court, probably truthfully, that when he raped his victims he felt no sexual desire, merely the need for omnipotence. We can only hope that these statements will have enlightened the courts about what it is that they are actually concerned with. Some thirty years ago, a German court ruled that the child murderer Jürgen Bartsch, himself the victim of extreme mental cruelty inflicted on him by his mother, should be castrated, in the hope that this operation would finally prevent him from living out his overly pronounced sexual drives on little children. What a grotesque, inhuman, and ignorant act![2]

The courts must finally realize that the force operative in the serial killing is in fact the desire for omnipotence felt by a child who has been disregarded, neglected, and reduced to impotence all his life. This has very little to do with sexuality, unless the feelings of impotence were bound up with experiences of incest.

Yet the question remains: Was there really no other way out for Patrice than to kill, to strangle these women as they whimpered and moaned? An independent observer will realize very quickly that it was his mother he was strangling over and over again in all these different women. In each case he was killing the person who had condemned him to such unspeakable torments as a child. He himself could hardly realize that fact. Hence he needed victims. Even today, he asserts that he loves his mother. Because there was no one to help him, no enlightened witness to stand by him and help him admit to himself, become aware of, and understand his death wishes toward his mother, those wishes proliferated inside him and forced him to kill other women instead of his mother.

"Is it as simple as that?" many psychiatrists will ask. My answer is yes—it is much simpler than what we have been forced to learn in order to honor our parents and not feel the hatred they deserve. But Patrice's hatred would not have killed anyone if he had experienced it at a conscious level. This hatred was the product of a much lauded attachment, the attachment to his mother, an attachment that drove him to murder. As a child he had only his mother to turn to for protection because living with his father was a constant source of mortal danger. How can a child living in nameless fear of his father afford to hate his mother as well—or at least to realize that he cannot expect any help from her? Such a child has to form an illusion and cling to that illusion. The price for that illusion was paid in this case by his victims. Feelings do not kill. The conscious experience of the disappointment caused by Patrice's mother, or even of the desire to strangle her, would not have killed anyone. It was the suppression of such a need, the disassociation of all the negative feelings unconsciously directed at his mother, that drove him to his terrible crimes.

13

Drugs and the
Deception of the Body

A S   A   C H I L D I had to learn to suppress my entirely natural responses to the injuries inflicted on me, responses
like rage, anger, pain, and fear. Otherwise I would have
been punished. Later, at school, I was proud of the skill I had
developed in controlling and restraining these feelings. I considered this ability a virtue, and I also expected my first child to
achieve the same kind of discipline. Only after I succeeded in
freeing myself of this attitude was I able to understand the sufferings of children who have been forbidden to respond to
injuries in an appropriate way and to engage with their emotions
in a benevolent environment, so that in later life they can take
their bearings from the feelings they actually have, rather than
fearing them.

Unfortunately, there are many people who have been through
the same thing as I have. Unable to display their strong feelings

as children, they have no real experience of them, and later they sorely miss this experience. In therapy, some of them succeed in locating and experiencing their repressed emotions. Then they are able to turn them into conscious feelings they can understand on the basis of their own life history and that they no longer need to fear. But others reject this course because they cannot or will not confide their tragic experiences to others. In our present-day consumer society such an attitude is widespread. It is considered the done thing not to display one's feelings, or only in exceptional cases, after the consumption of drugs or alcohol. Aside from that, feelings (one's own and those of others) are something to be jeered at. In show business and journalism the art of irony is a well-paid commodity, so it is possible to make a great deal of money with the suppression of one's feelings. Even if one ultimately risks losing all contact with oneself and merely functioning as a mask, an "as if" personality, there are always drugs, alcohol, and other substances to fall back on. Derision pays well; money is no object. Alcohol helps to keep us in a good mood, and stronger drugs do so even more effectively. But because these emotions are not genuine, not linked up with the true story of the body, the effect is bound to wear off after a time. Higher and higher doses are required to fill up the void left by childhood.

In an article published by *Der Spiegel online* (July 7, 2003), a successful young journalist tells the story of his yearlong addiction to heroin. I will quote various passages from this report, whose honesty and frankness affected me profoundly.

In some professions, taking drugs to boost one's creativity is thought to be a career asset. Managers, musicians, and other media stars resort to alcohol, cocaine, or heroin. An established journalist and chronic junkie reports on his addiction and the double life it entailed.

Two days before Christmas, I tried to strangle my girlfriend. Over the last few years, my life has repeatedly gone out of kilter in the weeks before and after the festive season. For fifteen years I had been trying to kick my heroin addiction, with varying success. I had made dozens of attempts and had been through two long-term inpatient therapies. For a few months, I had been injecting heroin on a daily basis, frequently in conjunction with cocaine.

This was how the young man maintained his equilibrium.

This time, things had gone well for about two years. I was writing for the most interesting newspapers in the country and earning good money. In the summer I had moved into a spacious apartment. And, most important, I was in love again. On this particular evening, shortly before Christmas, my girlfriend's body lay on the parquet floor, writhing beneath me, my hands at her throat.

A few hours before, I did everything I could to conceal those hands, though not because I had tried to strangle her. I was sitting in a hotel suite, interviewing one of Germany's most prominent theater directors. For some time I had had no choice but to inject the drug into the small veins on the backs of my hands and on my fingers. The veins on my arms were completely destroyed. In the meantime, my hands looked like the claws of some figure in a horror film, swollen, inflamed, punctured. I wore pullovers with very long sleeves. Luckily it was winter. The director had fine, shapely hands, hands that were constantly in motion, hands that played with my tape recorder when he was thinking what to say, hands with which he appeared to shape his own world.

I had difficulty concentrating on the interview. I had arrived by plane, and I had had my last shot many hours previously, before the flight. Smuggling heroin on board was too much of a risk. Anyway, I was trying to at least keep my consumption down to a certain level by buying only a limited amount every day. But at the end of the day things were getting tough. I became jumpy, constantly breaking out in a cold sweat. I wanted to go home. Right now. Concentrating my attention on something caused me actual physical effort. Somehow I got through the interview. If there was anything I feared more than the torments of withdrawal, it was the thought of losing my job. Ever since I was seventeen I had always dreamed of earning my money by writing. Ten years ago my dream came true. Sometimes it seemed as if my work was the last little bit of life that I had left.

All that remained was work. And work meant self-control. But where was his real life? Where were his feelings?

So I clung to my work. Every time I was given an assignment, the fear of not being up to it gnawed at my entrails. It was a mystery to me how I managed to cope with all the travel, conduct interviews, write articles.

So here I was in this hotel room, racked by fear of failure, shame, self-hate, and the craving for drugs. Only three-quarters of an hour more and you're through with it! I watched the director framing his sentences with eloquent gestures. A few hours later, I saw my own hands throttling my girlfriend.

Drugs may be able to suppress fear and pain so effectively that the person taking them does not have to confront his true feelings—as long as the effects of the drug are still potent. But those unlived emotions hit back all the more implacably when the effects start to wear off. And so it was here.

The return journey after the interview was sheer hell. In the taxi I lapsed into a shallow, feverish, exhausted sleep, repeatedly waking up from it in panic. A film of cold sweat covered my skin. It looked as if I would miss my plane. The thought of having to wait another hour and a half for my next shot was unbearable. Every ninety seconds I stared convulsively at my watch.

Addiction makes time your enemy. You're always waiting. Constantly, trapped in an endless time loop, over and over again. Waiting for the end of pain, for your dealer, for your next paycheck, for a place in a withdrawal clinic, or just for the day to end. For everything to come to an end. After every shot the clock is against you, mercilessly, inexorably.

Perhaps that is the most perfidious thing about addiction— it makes an enemy out of everything and everyone: time, your clamoring and craving body, friends and family whose worries you cannot dispel, a world that makes nothing but claims you feel you cannot live up to. Nothing structures life so implacably as addiction. It leaves no scope for doubt, not even for decisions. Satisfaction is a function of the amount of drugs available. Addiction regulates the world.

That afternoon I was only a few hundred miles from home, but it felt like the other side of the world. Home was where the drugs were waiting for me. The fact that I actually did get to the plane in time only gave me short-lived relief. The take-off was delayed; I lapsed back into stupor. Every time I opened my eyes and saw that the plane was still on the ground, I could have wept. The craving gradually pervaded my limbs and bit into my bones. Aches and pains in my arms and legs, as if my muscles and sinews were too short.

The banished emotions reassert themselves and invade the body.

Back at my apartment, Monika was waiting for me. That afternoon she had contacted our dealer, a young black man, and bought heroin and cocaine. That was the understanding between us—I earned the money, and she got the drugs.

I hated junkies; I wanted to have as little contact with the drug scene as possible. In my work, I limited my contact with editors to e-mails and faxes; I answered the phone only when the messages on the machine made it absolutely imperative. I had long since given up talking to my friends; I had nothing to say to them anyway.

As so often in the weeks before, I spent hours in the bathroom looking for a vein that was not completely destroyed. Cocaine devastates the veins; countless injections with unsterilized needles do the rest. My bathroom looked like a slaughterhouse, with smears of blood in the washbasin and on the floor, the walls and ceiling all spattered.

That day, I had fended off the worst withdrawal symptoms by smoking about a gram of heroin. The brown powder evaporates on the tray heated from below; you inhale the smoke as deeply as you can. As the drug goes through the lungs, you have to wait a few minutes before you feel the effects. An eternity. Slowly and gradually it envelops the mind, but the liberating kick refuses to come. A bit like sex without an orgasm.

Inhaling the stuff was torture for me—I have asthma. My lungs soon started rattling, and every breath stabbed me like a knife and gave me wrenching nausea. My panic increased with every fruitless injection attempt.

My mind was full of images, memories of moments full of unspeakable bliss, incredible intensity. Memories of how I learned to love hashish at the age of fourteen, because suddenly I didn't just hear music, I felt it with my whole body. Memories of how LSD got me standing in front of a pedestrian traffic signal, openmouthed with astonishment, as the changing colors triggered little explosions of light in my brain. Next to me my friends, all of us linked by a magical feeling of communion. Memories of my first shot, just as mind-blowing as the first experience of sex: the way the blend of heroin and cocaine set my nerve cells vibrating, a kind of huge Chinese gong made up of flesh and bone. Memories of the soothing effect of heroin, a kind of softening agent for the soul, envelop you in its warm embrace like the amniotic sac around a fetus. . . .

This young man gives us a graphic account of the power with which true needs and feelings return when drugs are not available. The authentic feelings of deficiency, abandonment, and rage produce a panic state, so that they have to be repelled with the aid of heroin. At the same time, the drug is used to manipulate the body into the "production" of desirable, positive feelings. Of course, the same mechanism is effective after the consumption of legal drugs, like prescribed medications or alcohol.

Compulsive substance addiction can have disastrous effects because it blocks off the path to genuine emotions and feelings. The drug can supply feelings of euphoria that reanimate the creativity scotched by a cruel upbringing. But the body will not tolerate this self-alienation for the duration of an entire life. In Kafka and others we have seen that creative activities like writing and painting can help one survive for a while, but they cannot restore access to the real source of human vitality forfeited through early abuse, at least not as long as one fears the discovery of one's true story.

Rimbaud is an especially harrowing example of this. Drugs were unable to act as a substitute for the emotional nourishment he really needed, and his body was not to be deceived about its true feelings. If he had met someone who could have helped him fully understand the destructive influence of his mother, he would no longer have needed to punish himself for it, and his life might have taken a different course. As it was, all his attempts to escape were doomed to failure, and he was constantly forced to return to his mother.

Like Rimbaud's, Paul Verlaine's life also came to a premature end, as we have learned. He died in misery at the age of fifty-one, due, on the face of it, to drug addiction and alcoholism that completely consumed his financial resources. But, as with so many others, the real cause was a lack of awareness and the self-subjection to a generally accepted commandment that forced him to endure without resistance his mother's control and manipulation (frequently with the help of money). Although in his younger years Verlaine had fervently hoped that he could free himself of his mother's control with the aid of self-manipulation and substance abuse, by the end he lived off women who gave him money, many of them prostitutes.

Drugs do not always have the function of freeing people from dependency and maternal constraints. Sometimes legal drugs (alcohol, nicotine, prescribed medications) are used in an attempt to fill the void left by the mother. The child was not given the nourishment needed from her and has found no substitute for this in later life. Without drugs, this gap can literally express itself as a feeling of physical hunger, gnawing away at the stomach, which contracts in response. Probably the foundations for addiction are laid at the very beginning of life, as is the case with bulimia and other eating disorders. The body makes it clear that in the past it urgently *needed* something, something withheld from it when it was a tiny baby. But this message is misunderstood as long as the emotions are ignored. Accordingly, the distress of the small child is erroneously registered as present distress, and all attempts to combat that distress in the present are doomed to failure. As adults we have different needs, and we can satisfy them only if they are no longer coupled with the old needs in our unconscious minds.

14

The Right to Awareness

A woman wrote to me saying that in years of therapy she attempted to forgive her parents for the sometimes dangerous physical attacks she was exposed to as a child. Subsequently her mother turned out to be psychotic. The more her daughter forced herself to adopt this forgiving attitude, the more profound her depression became. She felt as if she were locked up in a prison. Painting was the only thing that helped her fend off thoughts of suicide and stay alive. She arranged an exhibition and sold some of her work. The agents there gave her to understand that she had very good prospects for the future. Overjoyed at this, she told her mother the good news. Her mother's response was equally enthusiastic: "Now you'll be earning a lot of money and you'll be able to look after me."

When I read this, I was reminded of Clara, an acquaintance of mine. She once told me quite casually that, on the day she reached retirement age, which she had been looking forward to "like a new lease of life," her widowed father, a man in the best of health and with a high degree of business acumen, said, "Now at last you'll have time to help me run the firm." This woman had spent most of her life caring more for others than she had for herself. Thus, she was not even aware that this statement by her father represented a new and severe burden for her. She referred to it with a smile, almost cheerfully. The rest of her family also found that the time had come for her to take over the job left vacant by her father's longtime secretary, who had just died. Now, after all, she had time on her hands. What use would poor Clara make of her newfound freedom, if she did not sacrifice herself for the sake of her father? A few weeks later I heard that Clara had been taken ill with pancreatic cancer. She died shortly after. The whole time she had suffered severe pain, and my attempts to remind her of what her father had said were unsuccessful. She deplored the fact that her illness would now prevent her from being able to help him, as she loved him very much. She had no idea why this illness should have struck her down at this moment. She had never been ill; everyone had envied her excellent health. Clara lived in strict accordance with the conventions she had grown up with and obviously had very little awareness of her true feelings. When her body finally asserted itself, there was unfortunately no one in the family to help her identify what it was trying to tell her. Not even her adult children made any effort to do so, if they had in fact been able to.

The case of the painter I referred to earlier was very different. She was very clearly annoyed at her mother's reaction to the news that her pictures were selling well. She lost all pleasure in painting for a number of months and relapsed into her bouts of depression. Then she resolved to stop visiting her mother and also to avoid the friends who took the same view as her mother did. She stopped hiding her mother's condition from her acquaintances and started to communicate her true thoughts. More or less immediately, her energies were restored and she rediscovered her pleasure in painting. This renewal of her energies was brought about by the admission of the whole truth about her mother and the progressive withdrawal from attachment to her. This attachment was made up partly of compassion and partly of the expectation that she could make her mother happy and in so doing finally obtain the love she had never received before. But now she accepted the fact that she could never love her mother, and she also knew precisely why this was so.

Stories like this, with a positive ending, are still relatively rare. But I believe that in time there will be more and more of them, as we realize that we owe no gratitude, and certainly no sacrifices, to parents who abused us when we were small. These sacrifices are made for the sake of phantoms, idealized parents who have never existed. Why do we go on sacrificing ourselves for the sake of phantoms? Why do we remain the captives of relationships that remind us of the torments we went through when we were young? Because we hope that someday this will change, if we can find the magic word, assume the right attitude, achieve the right kind of understanding. But that would mean contorting ourselves in the same way as we did in our childhoods in the attempt to obtain love. Today, as adults, we know that our efforts were exploited, that this was not love in the true sense of the word. So why do we ultimately expect love from people who, for whatever reason, were unable to love us when we were small?

If we succeed in abandoning that hope, those expectations

will fall away, taking with them the self-deception that has been a constant factor in our lives. We no longer believe that we are not worth loving; we no longer believe we must prove that we are worthy of love after all. We are not to blame. It is the fault of the situation our parents found themselves in, what they made of the childhood traumas they themselves went through, the progress they made (or failed to make) in coming to terms with those traumas. There is nothing we can do to change all that. All we can do is live our own lives and change our attitudes accordingly. Most therapists believe that such changes of attitude can improve our relationships with our parents because the more mature attitude of adult children will prompt them to show those children more respect. This is not a belief that I can confirm with any certainty. My own experience suggests, on the contrary, that it is rare for positive changes in adult children to inspire admiration and satisfaction in the parents who were cruel to them in childhood. The opposite is in fact the case. The usual response is envy and withdrawal symptoms, accompanied by the expression of the wish that the son or daughter should be like he or she was before: submissive, unconditionally loyal, tolerant toward the cruel or dismissive treatment they came in for, and, in the last resort, depressed and unhappy. Increased awareness in adult children frightens many parents, and in the majority of cases there are no indications whatever of an improvement in the relationship. As my next example shows, however, this does happen sometimes.

A young woman who had long tormented herself with her feelings of hatred finally summoned up the courage to say to her mother, "I didn't like the mother you were to me when I was small. I hated you and I wasn't even aware of the fact." The woman was astonished that not only she herself but also her mother responded to this statement with relief. Deep down, both of them knew how they felt. Now the truth had finally been put into words. From then on, they could start building up a new and honest relationship.

Enforced love is not love. All it can lead to is a "sham" relationship without any genuine communication, a pretense of warmth and cordiality that does not really exist, a false avowal of affection designed to mask resentment or possibly even hatred. It can never lead to a genuine encounter. One of Mishima's works is called *Confessions of a Mask*. How can a mask genuinely relate what the person behind it has experienced? It cannot. The story it tells in Mishima's work is purely intellectual. All Mishima could do was to relate the consequences of the facts, but both these facts and the emotions that went with them remained inaccessible to his conscious mind. The consequences manifested themselves in pathological, perverted fantasies, what we might call an "abstract death wish." The actual feelings of a little child imprisoned in his grandmother's room year after year were beyond the reach of the adult he finally became.

Relationships based on masklike communication of this kind cannot change. They remain what they have always been: instances of *mis*-communication. A genuine relationship is possible only if both partners can admit their feelings, experience them and communicate them to each other without fear. It is fine and uplifting when this happens. But it is rare, because both partners' fear of giving up the accustomed façade or mask prevents any genuine exchange.

Why should we seek this exchange with our old parents, of all people? They are no longer partners for us, in the genuine sense of the word. The story that linked us with them is over once we have children of our own and once we can genuinely communicate with partners we have selected for ourselves. The peace that so many people crave is not something that can be bestowed from the outside. Many therapists believe we can find peace through forgiveness, but this opinion is constantly refuted by the facts. We know that priests intone the Lord's Prayer every day, which means that they pray for forgiveness, both for their own "trespasses" and for those who sin against us. But this does not prevent some of them from yielding to the repeated compulsion to abuse children and young people, while repressing the fact that they are committing a crime. In so doing, they are also protecting their own parents and they have no awareness of the crimes those parents committed on them. Accordingly, I believe that preaching forgiveness is not only hypocritical and futile but also actively dangerous. It masks the compulsion to repeat.

The only thing that can protect us from repetition is the admission of the truth—the whole truth, with all its implications. Once we know as accurately as possible what our parents did to us, we are no longer in danger of repeating their misdeeds. Otherwise we will do so automatically, and with all the tenacity at our disposal we will resist the idea that we can—and indeed must—break off our infant attachment to parents who abused us if we want to become adults and live a life of our own in peace. We must give up the confusion we lived in as infants, the confusion stemming from our early attempts to understand abuse and give it a meaning. As adults we can do that; we can learn to understand how morality in therapy gets in the way of the healing of the wounds we carry around inside us.

Here are some examples of how this awareness can develop. A young woman was in despair because she believed herself to be a failure, both in her job and in her personal relationships. She wrote:

> The more my mother tells me I'm hopeless, someone who can never get anywhere, the more I fail at everything I do. I don't want to hate my mother, I want to make peace with her, forgive her, so that I can finally be rid of my hatred. But I can't. In my hatred I feel hunted by her, as if she hated me. But that cannot be true. What have I done wrong? I know that I will suffer if I cannot manage to forgive her. My therapist told me that if I am at war with my parents, it is the same as if I were at war with myself. Of course I know that we cannot forgive if we cannot forgive from the bottom of our hearts. I feel deeply confused. There are times when I can forgive, when I feel compassion for my parents. Then my rage returns, I rebel at the thought of what they did to me, and I do not want to see them. I want to live my own life, to be at peace and not to think all the time about how they hit me and humiliated me and almost tortured me.

This woman was convinced that she was in a state of war with her parents. Her therapist had told her that, when she took her memories seriously and remained true to what her body tells her, it was the same as being at war with herself. The consequence of that statement was that this woman could not distinguish between her own life and the life of her parents, that she had no identity of her own and could see herself only as part of her parents. How could a therapist say such a thing? I have no idea. But I believe that a statement like this betrays the therapist's own fear of *her* parents. It is small wonder that the patient should be infected by this fear and confusion. As a result, she will not dare

to discover the story of her own childhood and let her body live
with the truth.

In another instance, a highly intelligent woman wrote that she
did not intend any blanket condemnation of her parents. Even
though she had been beaten and sexually abused as a child, she
also experienced some good times with them. Her therapist
encouraged her to weigh up the good times against the bad and
told her that as an adult she must understand that perfect parents simply do not exist, that all parents make mistakes. But this
is not the point. The point is that this adult woman needed to
develop empathy for the little girl she had once been, the little
girl whose sufferings went unnoticed, who was used for the
interests of her parents and who thanks to her unusual gifts was
consummately good at living up to these expectations, although
no one spared her sufferings so much as a thought. If she had
now reached a stage where she could feel that suffering and be
a true companion to the child within, the last thing she should
do is to weigh up the good moments against the bad. In doing so,
she will relapse into the role of the little girl doing her best to
comply with her parents' wishes—loving them, forgiving them,
remembering the good times, etc.

As a child she did this all the time, in the hope of understanding the conflicting messages and actions her parents exposed
her to. But this inner "work" confused her even more. It was
completely impossible for the child to understand that her
mother had retreated inside an inner fortress designed to guard
against the experience of her own feelings and hence had no
sensitivity whatsoever for the needs of her child. And if she
understands that as an adult, she should not persist in the
child's hopeless expectations, she should not try to arrive at an

objective assessment, weigh up the good against the bad. She should act on her own feelings, which, like everything emotional, are fully and entirely subjective. She should ask herself "What tormented me in my childhood? What did I not allow myself to feel?"

Such questions will enable her to identify with the perspective of the suffering, speechless child and the discontinuation of an attachment that I believe to be destructive. As I have said, this attachment is made up of gratitude, compassion, denial, longing, euphemism, and a host of expectations that will always remain unfulfilled. The path to adulthood lies not in tolerance for the cruelties we have been exposed to but in the realization of our own truth and the development of empathy for the maltreated child. It lies in the appreciation of the way in which cruelties have handicapped our whole lives as adults, the way in which so many opportunities have been destroyed and so much misery passed on unintentionally to the next generation. This tragic realization is only possible if we stop weighing the good points of our parents against the bad. If we persist in doing that, we will relapse into compassion, into the denial of the cruelties we have been subjected to, all because we believe we must take a "balanced" view of things. My conviction is that this reflects the efforts undertaken by the children we once were. The adult perspective must reject this balancing process because it is confusing and gets in the way of our own lives. Of course, people who were never beaten in childhood, who were never subjected to sexual abuse, do not need to do this work. They can enjoy the good feelings they have in the company of their parents, they can quite rightly call them love, and they do not need to deny themselves in any way. The burden of such "work" weighs on individuals who have been abused and then only if they are not willing to pay for self-deception with physical illness.

For example, a woman has read on the Internet that we cannot truly help ourselves by breaking off contact with our parents. If we do that, we will feel constantly pursued by them. She writes to the forum on my Web site, saying that this squares precisely with her own experience. Ever since she stopped visiting her parents she has been thinking of them night and day and lives in a state of permanent anxiety. This is very understandable. The reason she lives in a constant state of panic is that the alleged experts on the Internet have reinforced her fear of her parents. The morality they subscribe to insists that an individual has no right to his/her own life, feelings, and needs. I assume that there is very little else to be found on the Internet, because the Internet is a faithful reflection of a mentality we have sustained for thousands of years. Its message is: Honor your parents and you will live long.

The thumbnail biographies of world-famous writers in Part I showed that this is not always the case, particularly if the individuals in question are sensitive and gifted. But a long life is no indication in itself that the threat implicit in the Fourth Commandment is justified. Quite the contrary. The length of life tells us nothing about the quality of that life. The central point at issue here is that parents and grandparents should be aware of their responsibility, that they should not honor their ancestors at the expense of their children and grandchildren, whom they uncaringly subject to sexual abuse, beatings, or other forms of cruelty that are alleged to be good for them. It is true that parents can take the strain off their own bodies by taking out on their children the powerful feelings directed deep down at their own parents. But they can also fall ill very quickly when those children withdraw from them, at least outwardly.

Today's children and grandchildren are entitled to be aware, they are entitled to believe what they saw and felt as children. They need not force themselves into blindness. They have paid for such enforced blindness with physical or mental disorders whose real causes have remained concealed for so long. If they stop conniving in such concealment, they will have a real prospect of freeing themselves of the chains of violence and self-deception, and then they will no longer claim sacrifices from their own children.

Recently I saw a program on television showing children with neurodermatitis, a tormenting condition that involves a permanent itching all over the body. The experts interviewed stated flatly that this condition is incurable. No mention was made of possible psychic causes for it. The striking thing was that the condition of these children improved, and in some cases disappeared altogether, when they met other children in hospital suffering from the same disorder. It seemed obvious to me that such encounters had a remedial effect because they gave the children the feeling that they were not alone with this mysterious symptom.

Shortly afterward, I met Veronica, a woman who developed neurodermatitis during psychotherapy and realized in the course of time that this very symptom made it possible for her to terminate her early, fateful attachment to her father. Veronica was the youngest of five children and was sexually exploited by her older sisters. Her mother was an alcoholic, and Veronica experienced her mother's unexpected outbursts of rage as a threat to her own existence. In this situation the little girl desperately clung to the hope that her father would come to her rescue. Veronica idealized her father all her life, although there was no reason or memory that would justify such a high assessment of his character. He too was an alcoholic, and the only interest he showed in all his daughters was purely sexual. But Veronica denied this reality, she adhered to her irrational hope and upheld that illusion for fifty years. During therapy she experienced severe attacks of itching whenever she encountered people to whom she could not make herself understood and from whom she expected help.

Veronica told me that it had long been a mystery to her why she was constantly plagued by this itching and could do nothing about it, except fly into a rage when the temptation to scratch herself became too strong. It later transpired that this eruption of her flesh was an expression of the rage she felt at her whole family, and most notably at her father, who was never there when she needed him, although she had dreamed up the role of savior for him so as to bear the loneliness she felt in a family that did nothing but abuse her. Of course, the fact that this rescue fantasy lasted for fifty years only made her rage all the greater. But with the help of her therapist she finally discovered that the itching always started whenever she tried to suppress a feeling. It left her no peace until she was able to admit and experience that feeling. Thanks to her feelings, she finally became more and more clearly aware of the fact that she had built up a fantasy around her father that had no basis in fact. She was waiting for her beloved father to protect her against her mother and sisters and to understand her distress. From an external viewpoint, the fact that this was never going to happen would be as clear as day. But for Veronica herself such a realistic view was absolutely inconceivable; she felt she would die if she ever admitted the truth.

This is understandable. Inside her body the unprotected child lived on, the child who would have been doomed to die without the illusion that her father would ultimately come to her aid. As an adult Veronica was able to give up this illusion because the child was no longer alone with her fate. From now on, there existed within her an adult part that was able to protect her, to assume the role the father had never assumed, to understand the child's distress and guard her from abuse. She experienced this repeatedly in her everyday life, once she was able to stop ignoring the needs of her body and to take them seriously. Later, her body signaled these needs with a slight itch, warning her that the child within needed her support. Although Veronica had a responsible job, she had tended to form attachments to people who did not care for her at all and finally to become totally dependent on them. This stopped as soon as she saw her father's behavior for what it was. After therapy, there was a complete change in this regard. In her body she found an ally that knew exactly how she could help herself. In my view, this is precisely what the aim of psychotherapy should be.

If therapy is to be successful, the species of morality implicit in the Fourth Commandment, something inculcated into us at a very early stage in our upbringing, has to be dethroned. In far too many therapies, the morality of poisonous pedagogy either rules triumphant from the outset, or else rears its head in the later course of events because the therapist has not been able to shake off these constraints. Even in cases where, for a time, the client has been given genuine help in finally recognizing the injuries and cruelties he/she has been subjected to, there comes a point sooner or later when the therapist suggests that at least one of the parents had a good side and gave the child a great deal that the adult should now be grateful for. Such a suggestion is sufficient to cast the client into a state of total confusion, because it is precisely this concern to see the parents' good sides that has led to the disorder in question, to the repression of perceptions and feelings so impressively described by Imre Kertész in *Fateless*.

A woman I shall call Laura wrote to me saying that she had engaged in a course of psychotherapy with someone who, initially at least, enabled her for the first time to put aside the mask she had been hiding behind. She was able to recognize that her own harshness was artificial and to place her trust in a person who helped her to find access to her own feelings and recall her infant longing for closeness and tenderness. Like Veronica, Laura had turned to her father for protection against her mother's coldness. Her father had shown much more interest than had been the case with Veronica. He sometimes played with her, thus sustaining her hopes for a good relationship. But although this father had known about the vicious corporal punishment meted out to Laura by her mother, he still left her in her care, did nothing to protect her, and finally abandoned her altogether without assuming any responsibility for the child. The worst thing was that he had aroused in the child a love that he did not deserve. The young woman lived with this love until she came down with a serious illness, a uterine tumor whose meaning she attempted to discover with the help of various therapists. The last of these therapists made a very promising impression. With his help, Laura succeeded in breaking down the wall of defense she had erected within herself. But when Laura began to express suspicions that her father may have sexually abused her, the therapist himself started putting up a wall. Suddenly he started talking about oedipal wishes on the child's part and plunged her into the same state of confusion as the one caused by her father. She suspected that he sacrificed her to his own weakness, maybe to his own repressed memories he had not come to terms with. But she didn't dare tell him what she felt.

Because she was very well read, Laura thought that she was able to see through the therapist's defense. But because her relationship with her father was still unresolved, she repeated the same pattern with the therapist. She could not share her doubts with him; she remained grateful for the good her father and her therapist had done her, remained obedient, and was unable to break off her infant attachment in either case. Accordingly, the symptoms persisted, despite the primal therapy she tried next. Morality appeared to have won the day, because she sacrificed both her personal history and her sufferings to it, as happens in so many cases of psychotherapy. Later, in group therapy, Laura was able to realize that her gratitude was groundless. She realized how her father had failed her in her childhood; she grasped all the consequences ensuing from that failure and understood that it was up to her to shoulder the responsibility for living her own life.

From then on, she was able to lead a new, creative life, because she had finally admitted her own personal truth. She knew now that she had nothing to fear as long as she allowed herself to be aware that her father was quite simply a weakling who never helped her because he never wanted to. He had needed her for the abreaction of his own injuries so that he could avoid having to actually feel them. Laura's body was pacified by this new awareness. The tumor, which the doctors had insisted must be operated on without delay, disappeared very quickly.

In one of her earlier therapies, Laura had been offered the visualization method and had pinned all her hopes to it. She succeeded in recalling a scene that had happened when she was seventeen, in which her idealized father had struck her in a fit of jealousy. Her therapist told her she should try to imagine her father as kind and friendly and to substitute this positive image for the negative one. This did indeed help Laura to maintain the idealization of her father for a few more years. In that time, the tumor in her uterus continued to grow until she finally resolved to confront the truth indicated by her genuine memory.

TECHNIQUES OF THIS kind are used in therapy for the explicit purpose of changing negative feelings into positive ones. Usually, however, such manipulation merely serves to reinforce the denial that has enabled clients to avoid facing up to the pain of their own truth, a truth indicated by authentic emotions. Accordingly, the success achieved by these methods can be of only short duration, and the whole approach is highly problematic. The original negative emotion is an important signal emitted by the body. If that message is ignored, the body has to emit new signals in an attempt to make itself heard.

Artificially induced positive feelings are not only short-lived, they also leave us in the state of a child hoping against hope that our parents will one day show their good sides, thus relieving us of the necessity to feel anger or fear in connection with them. But if we want to attain true adulthood and live in our present reality, we must (and can) free ourselves of these illusory expectations. To do so, we need to admit the so-called negative emotions and change them into meaningful feelings, instead of trying to banish them as quickly and effectively as possible. Once they

are admitted into our awareness, these emotions do not last for-
ever, though in the relatively short time they persist they can liberate pent-up energies. Only when we attempt to ignore or
banish them altogether do they ensconce themselves in the body.

Relaxation, massage, and various kinds of body therapy can
bring major temporary respite by freeing muscles and connective
tissue from the pressure of repressed emotions, by easing tension
and thus relieving pain. But this pressure will reassert itself if we
refuse to identify the causes of these emotions, if the child
within us still harbors a strong anticipation of punishment, and
if, for that reason, we fear angering our parents or the persons
who have taken their place.

Equally ineffectual in the long term are the frequently recommended exercises of "letting out" or "working off" our anger by
means of such expedients as pillow fights or boxing, as long as we
are forced to take a lenient attitude to those persons who caused
our anger in the first place. Laura tried out many such exercises,
invariably with short-lived success. Only when she was ready to
perceive the full extent of her disappointment at her father and
to feel not only the anger but also the pain and the fear it had
caused did her uterus free itself of the tumor without any
recourse to relaxation exercises or the like.

15

Deception Kills Love

IN ONE OF his books (published in German as *Ich werde es sagen* by Klett Verlag in 2003, not available in English), the young Danish writer Kristian Detlev Jensen describes his experiences at the hands of a pedophile from age nine to twelve. Jensen's horrifying narrative indicates very clearly the lingering effects of such abuse. The events were so traumatic that he could not bring himself to inform the police until he reached adulthood. Although Kristian's account left the police in no doubt about the true circumstances and although others had been molested in the same way, the verdict passed on the offender was a suspended sentence and two years' probation. Understandably, this injustice left the young man in a highly agitated state. Despite years of therapy he was unable to sleep, had difficulty in concentrating, suffered terrifying nightmares and was subject to frequent bouts of panic that he was unable to control.

What prevents an only child of above-average intelligence from telling his parents how dreadfully he has suffered over a three-year period? Kristian's parents lived in the Danish provinces and sent him to Copenhagen once a week to enjoy himself. We are told they never suspected that the boy was sexually abused every weekend by the man they asked to look after him in the capital. How can we explain the fact that the boy tolerated this interference although he was undoubtedly repelled by it? Why was he unable to extricate himself from the grip of his tormentor by talking to his parents about what he was going through? If he did not keep the matter secret, he would have to face the crippling boredom of life in the provinces with his parents and a total absence of empathy, understanding, interest, and communication. He believed he had found all these things in the shape of Gustav, his "friend." He reveled in the stimulating life of Copenhagen where, thanks to Gustav, he was able to go to concerts, restaurants, the theater, and the cinema. The full panoply of cultural life in the capital was his for the asking. Accordingly, he did his best to accept the slavery he was subjected to in Gustav's bed, to forget it in the course of the day, to enjoy the world of culture he now had access to, and to ignore the bad side of the deal.

But things did not work out like that. Kristian's body rebelled in a variety of ways because of the infinite rage within him, a rage that could never be expressed, either to Gustav himself or to Kristian's parents. While the book reveals that the parents' indifference was in fact the ground in which sexual abuse was able to take root and flourish, the author insists in his preface that today he loves his parents dearly and has forgiven them for absolutely everything.

It was this sentence that I found most significant, as it illustrates the covert, but nonetheless virulently destructive power of the Fourth Commandment. As a child Kristian was unable to free himself of Gustav's pernicious influence because he believed that he could not live without the joys of the capital to which Gustav had introduced him. If he were forced to return to the soul-destroying boredom of his parents' provincial home, then he would surely die. Accordingly he submitted to his "friend's" brainwashing and chose to ignore the obvious abuse to which he was being subjected. Today, as an adult, he can see what harm was done to him, and for that reason he is no longer forced to love Gustav. But the ties that link him to his parents have lost none of their power. And this is what Kristian Jensen calls love.

Kristian's account indicates very clearly that the unquestioning obedience drilled into him by his parents and the neglect with which they treated him paved the way for the crimes perpetrated on him by this pedophile. He acquits his parents of any kind of responsibility for his dilemma. The reader can sense Kristian's adult indignation at the behavior of his parents, who calmly entrusted him to the care of a criminal every weekend for a period of three years. But the child within cannot venture to feel this disgust; the fear of his parents is still too overpowering. This may explain why Kristian still suffers from his symptoms. His rage at Gustav's behavior is legitimate because the contempt for pedophiles is shared by society. But the rage caused by his parents is forbidden and goes unrecognized. This forbidden resentment must stay pent up in his body—it produces nightmares and other symptoms because it is not accessible to his adult consciousness. What remains is the longing for "good" parents, and this longing sustains all the illusions he entertains about them.

Kristian Jensen is no exception. I constantly receive books by authors relating inconceivable cruelties perpetrated on them in their early years. However, on the very first pages of these books they assure the reader that they have forgiven their parents for everything done to them. All these cases are a sure indication of compulsive repetition, the compulsion to prolong the deception they were once subjected to. This compulsion manifests itself above all in the assertion that forgiveness has a salutary effect.

Can forgiveness for the crimes done to a child be not just ineffective but actively harmful? It certainly can because the body does not understand moral precepts. It fights to make our conscious minds admit the truth and transcend our denial of genuine feelings. This is something children cannot afford to do. They have to deceive themselves and turn a blind eye to their parents' crimes in order to survive. Adults no longer need to repress their feelings. But if they do, the price they pay is high. Either they ruin their own health or they make others foot the bill.

A therapist who has forgiven his parents for the cruelty they showed him may feel the urge to suggest this same remedy to his clients. In so doing, he is exploiting their dependence and their trust. If he is not in touch with his own feelings at all, he may indeed be unaware that he is doing to others what was once done to him. In suggesting forgiveness as a solution, the therapist is abusing and confusing others, while rejecting any kind of responsibility for his actions. He is convinced that he is acting for their own good. Are not all religions unanimous in their conviction that forgiveness is the path to heaven? Was not Job ultimately rewarded for the fact that he forgave God?

Unlike children, adult patients have a choice. They can leave a therapist once they have seen through his deception and self-deception. They need not identify with him and repeat his acts all over again. As an adult, Kristian Jensen is free to see through Gustav's manipulations. Accordingly he is hardly in danger of doing the same to others. But a child does not have this freedom. Children cannot escape their own parents, so they cannot afford to see through them either. Blindness makes it possible to survive. This is the way the abuse of children has functioned since time immemorial. *Blindness and forgiveness are essential to survival.* But at the same time they lead to repetition and they perpetuate cycles of cruelty.

To break through this vicious circle we need to understand that so-called love cannot survive abuse, deception, and exploitation without seeking new victims. And if it requires new victims, it is no longer love but at best the longing for love. Only unflinching realization of one's own past reality, of what really happened can break through the chain of abuse. If I know and can feel what my parents did to me when I was totally defenseless, I no longer need victims to befog my awareness. I no longer need to reenact what happened to me and take it out on innocent people because now I *know* what happened. And if I want to live my life consciously, without exploiting others, then I must actively accept that knowledge.

No Communication

III

ANOREXIA: THE LONGING FOR GENUINE COMMUNICATION

... because I could not find the food
that appeals to me.
If I had found it, believe me,
I would have made no fuss
and eaten my fill like you
and everyone else.

    —*Franz Kafka*, A Hunger Artist

THE AREA IN which morality celebrates its greatest triumphs is the treatment of anorexia. Here it is almost the rule for the guilt feelings of young anorexics to be aggravated by more or less blatant injunctions like "Look how unhappy you are making your parents, how they suffer on your account!" The meaning of their refusal of nourishment, the message it is trying to get across, is completely ignored in such harangues. Yet anorexia shows us very clearly how definite the body can be in indicating the personal truth of its "owner."

Many anorexics think, "I have to love and honor my parents, forgive them for everything they have done, understand them, think positive, learn to forget. I have to do this and do that. I must not show my distress."

But what is left of me—the real me—if I try to force myself to have feelings I do not really have, if I no longer know what I really feel, want, need, and why I should do all the things that people tell me to do? I can force myself to achieve—at work, in sports, in everyday life. But if I force alien feelings on myself (with or without the aid of substances like alcohol, drugs, and medication), I shall be confronted sooner or later with the consequences of this self-deception. I reduce myself to a mask and do not know who I really am. The source of that knowledge lies in my genuine feelings; those feelings correspond with my experiences. And the guardian of those experiences is my body. Its memory.

We cannot love, respect, or understand ourselves if we ignore the messages of our body, as expressed in feelings like anger. There are a whole range of "therapeutic" rules and techniques for the manipulation of feelings. They tell us in all seriousness how we can stop suffering and start enjoying life. People with the severest physical symptoms go to hospitals for this kind of advice, in the hope that it will help them free themselves from the nagging resentment they harbor against their parents.

This may succeed for a while and also bring relief, because then their therapists are "pleased" with them. Like good little children complying with their mothers' parenting methods, they then feel accepted and loved. But sometime later the body will reassert itself with a relapse, the retaliation for the refusal to listen to what it has to say.

THERAPISTS HAVE SIMILAR difficulty dealing with the symptoms displayed by hyperactive children. How can these children be integrated into their families if their condition is regarded as a genetic quirk or as an instance of obstinate naughtiness that needs to be drummed out of them by corrective measures? And all to ensure that the true causes remain undiscovered? But if we are willing to see that these emotions have a basis in reality, that they are reactions to neglect, abuse, or a lack of nourishing communication, then we will see not just children who cannot sit still but children who are suffering and are not allowed to know why. If *we* permit ourselves this knowledge, we can help them and ourselves. Perhaps we (and they) fear not so much the emotions, the pain, the fear, and the anger, but rather the knowledge of what our parents have done to us.

The (moral) obligation supported by most therapists to refrain at all costs from apportioning blame to our parents leads to voluntary ignorance about the causes of an illness and hence about the possibilities of treating that illness. Experts on the human brain have known for some years that the absence of a resilient attachment to the mother in the period up to the third year of life leaves decisive traces in the brain and leads to severe disorders. It is indeed time that this knowledge is imparted to people training to be therapists. This might be one way of reducing the harmful influences of their traditional upbringing. For it is often our upbringing, the legacy of poisonous pedagogy, that has prohibited us from querying our parents' deeds. Conventional morality, religious injunctions, and, not least, some psychoanalytic theories are also operative in causing even child therapists to flinch from identifying the parents' responsibility and calling it by name. Their fear of causing parents feelings of guilt is disguised as a fear that, if therapists did so, the parents might harm the child.

I am convinced that the opposite is the case. Addressing the truth can open clients' eyes, once a therapeutic rapport has been established. Of course, a child therapist cannot change the parents of a "disturbed" child, but he can do a lot to improve their relationship with the child if he supplies them with the requisite knowledge. If, for example, he informs them of the *nourishing* significance of genuine communication and helps them to make use of that knowledge, he will give them access to new experiences. Frequently, parents withhold such communication from the child, not because they are in any way malevolent but because they themselves never experienced such a token of affection in childhood and consequently do not know that such a thing exists. They can learn to communicate meaningfully with their children, but only if those children have the full support of a therapist who has shaken off the influence of poisonous pedagogy and is totally and unreservedly on the children's side.

With the support of the enlightened witness represented by such a therapist, a hyperactive child (or a child suffering from any other disorder) can be encouraged to feel its perturbation, rather than acting it out, and to articulate its feelings to the parents, rather than fearing them and disassociating from them. In this way, the parents can learn *from the child* that one can have feelings without needing to fear disastrous consequences, that, on the contrary, something can develop from this which gives support and creates mutual trust.

I know of one mother who was actually able to escape from the destructive attachment to her parents thanks to her own child. After several years of therapy, she was still concerned to see the good sides of her parents even though she had been severely abused by them in her childhood. She suffered greatly from the hyperactivity and the aggressive outbursts of her little daughter, who had been under continual medical care since birth. The routine had been the same for years. She took her child to the doctor, gave her the medicine prescribed for her,

went to see her therapist regularly, and went on seeking justifica-
tions for her own parents. At a conscious level, she never suffered because of her parents' treatment of her, only because of
her daughter. One day, however, she finally flew into a rage in the
company of a new therapist and was finally able to admit to the
extreme anger at her parents that had been pent up inside her for
thirty years. And then a miraculous thing happened (although it
was anything but a miracle): in the space of a few days, her
daughter started to play normally, lost all her symptoms, asked
questions, and was given straightforward answers. It was as if the
mother had emerged from a dense fog and was seeing her daughter properly for the first time. A child who is not being used as
the object of projections can play quietly without having to run
around like mad all the time. She no longer has the hopeless task
of saving her mother, or at least of confronting her with the truth
by means of her own "disorder."

Genuine communication is based on facts; it enables people
to tell others about their thoughts and feelings. By contrast, confusing communication is based on the distortion of the facts and
blaming others for the unwanted emotions that are actually
directed at one's childhood parents. This kind of manipulative
communication is the only form known to poisonous pedagogy.
Until recently it was ubiquitous, but now there are exceptions, as
the following example shows.

Seven-year-old Mary refused to go to school after her teacher
hit her. Her mother, Flora, was in despair; after all she could not
force the child to go to school. She herself had never hit her
daughter. She visited the teacher, confronted her with the situation, and asked her to apologize to the child. The teacher reacted
indignantly. A fine state of affairs it would be if teachers were to

start apologizing to their pupils! She insisted that Mary had deserved to be hit because she had not listened when spoken to. Flora retorted quietly, "A child who does not listen to you may be afraid of the tone in your voice or the expression on your face. Blows will only add to that fear. Instead of resorting to blows, it would be better to talk to the child, gain her confidence and in that way dispel the tension and the fear."

Suddenly tears formed in the teacher's eyes. She slumped onto her chair and whispered, "Blows were all I ever got as a child; no one ever talked to me. I can still hear my mother shouting at me, 'You never listen—what am I going to do with you?' "

Flora suddenly felt compassion. She had come with the intention of telling the teacher that physical correction has long been prohibited in school and that she would be reporting her to the police. But now, on the chair in front of her sat an authentic person she could genuinely address. Finally the two women tried to work out a way of regaining little Mary's confidence. The teacher offered to apologize and actually did so. She explained to Mary that she had nothing more to fear because hitting pupils is not allowed and she, the teacher, had done something wrong. She told her that in such a case Mary has a right to complain, because teachers sometimes make mistakes too. After that, Mary went back to school quite happily and even took a liking to this woman who had had the courage to admit her mistake.

With this experience, a child like Mary will not feel responsible for the emotions of others, as so many people do, but only for her own. The child will have sensed that the emotions of adults depend on their own biographies and are not caused by the behavior of the children in their charge. If their behavior and helplessness trigger strong emotions in the adults dealing with them, the children need not feel guilty about it, even if those adults attempt to blame it on them ("I hit you *because you . . .*").

16

The Fictional Diary
of Anita Fink

A MONG THE MANY letters and diaries sent to me are numerous accounts of cruelty and abuse in childhood. There are also (though these are more rare) reports of therapies that have helped the writers to resolve the consequences of their traumatic childhood. Sometimes people ask me to publish these life histories, but in most cases I am reluctant to do so because I do not know whether the individuals concerned will relish finding themselves in someone else's book a few years later.

In that light, I have resolved to write a narrative that, though fictional, is based on facts. I believe that many people carry a similar suitcase filled with shame and suffering around with them without ever having had the good fortune of experiencing successful therapy. Here, a young woman I have called Anita Fink recounts the development in her therapy that helped her to free herself of one of the cruelest disorders: anorexia.

Even among the more traditionally minded representatives of the medical profession it is generally acknowledged that anorexia is a psychosomatic disorder. When a (usually young) individual loses so much weight that her life is in danger, then we can be sure that her mind is "affected." But such light as has been cast on the psychic condition of these people usually remains diffuse. In my view, the reason for this denial is again obedience to the Fourth Commandment.

I have already touched on this problem in *The Truth Will Set You Free*, although there I did no more than to rail against conventional methods of treatment for anorexia, which concentrate on getting the patient's weight back to normal, rather than casting genuine light on the causes of the disorder. Instead of reverting to this polemic, I want here to use a narrative to illustrate the psychic factors leading to anorexia and to indicate the measures that can overcome this condition.

At the end of his life, Kafka's hunger artist says the reason he refused to eat was that he never found the kind of nourishment that appealed to him. This is something that Anita herself might have said—but only after she regained her health, because only then did she know what nourishment she needed, what she had been looking for, what she had missed ever since her childhood: genuine emotional communication, without lies, without false "concerns," without guilt feelings, without reproaches, without intimidation, without projections. This is a form of communication that in the ideal case exists in the first stages of life between the mother and the child she has borne because the mother really wanted it. If this has never taken place, if the child has been fed with lies, if words and gestures have served only to disguise the rejection of the child, to mask hatred, repulsion, disgust, then the child will refuse to thrive on this "nourishment." She will reject it and later become anorexic without knowing what nourishment she really needs. As she has no experience of it, she does not know that it exists.

As adults, such individuals may have a vague inkling that such nourishment does exist and may indulge in orgies of eating, stuffing themselves indiscriminately with all kinds of food in the quest for something they need but do not know. The result is obesity and bulimia. They do not want to go without; they want to eat, to gorge themselves without restrictions. However, like anorexics, they do not know what they need, so they can never eat their fill. They want to be free to eat whatever they like, free of all restrictions. But ultimately they are the victims of their compulsive guzzling. To free themselves of this compulsion they need to be able to share their feelings with someone—they need the experience of being listened to, understood, taken seriously, of no longer having to hide. Only then will they know that this is the nourishment they have been searching for all their lives.

Kafka's hunger artist could not put a name to it because Kafka himself could not put a name to it. As a child he was deprived of genuine communication. He suffered unspeakably from this deficiency, and all his works describe nothing other than miscommunication, be it *The Castle*, *The Trial*, or *The Metamorphosis*. In all these novels and stories the questions are never heard—they are answered with strange distortions, and the central figures are totally isolated, totally incapable of getting someone to listen.

For a long time Anita Fink had the same problem. The true source of her illness was the unfulfilled longing for communication, the deprivation of genuine contact with her parents and boyfriend. Her refusal to eat was the sign of this deficiency. Ultimately her recovery was possible because Anita realized that there were people who could and did understand her.

In September 1997, our fictional Anita, then sixteen years old and hospitalized, started keeping a diary.

September 15, 1997

Well, they've done it. My weight is more like what it should be and I've started to hope. But why do I say "they've done it"? It wasn't them at all. In this awful hospital they got on my nerves from the very beginning, it was worse than being at home. "Do this, do that, no, you can't do that, who do you think you are, we're trying to help you but you've got to have faith and obey, otherwise no one can help you."

Where do you get your bloody arrogance from? Why should I get better just because I tie in with your stupid system and function like a cog in your machine? That would kill me. And I don't want to die! You keep on saying I want to die, but it's a lie, complete and utter nonsense. I want to live, but not the way other people tell me to, just so they can prevent me from dying. I want to live as the person I really am. But they won't let me. No one lets me. They all have designs on me. And what they're really doing is snuffing out my life with those designs. I wanted to tell you that, but how could I? How can you tell people that, if they come in to the hospital because it's their job, people who only want successes to report on ("Anita, have you eaten your roll today?"), people who are glad to get out of here in the evening, to leave wraiths like me behind and go home and listen to some music?

I really feel no one listens to me. That nice doctor pretends that listening is the purpose of his visit. But his real aims are

entirely different, I can tell by the way he jollies me along, trying to give me the courage to live (how can you "give" someone that?), explaining that everyone here is trying to help me,
that my illness is sure to go away if I start trusting them, that
in fact my illness is due to my not trusting anyone. But I'll
learn that here, in time. Then he looks at his watch and
thinks what an impression his report on this case will make at
the seminar this evening. He has found the key to anorexia:
trust. You ass! What were you thinking of when you started
preaching trust at me? They all preach trust, but none of
them deserve it. You say you want to listen to me, but all you
do is try to impress me, you want to fool me, you want me to
like you, admire you, and you want to get something out of
this whole business: you want to be able to tell your col-
leagues how clever you were in getting an intelligent woman
to trust you.

You conceited bastard, I've seen through your game at last.
You won't fool me again. If I'm a bit better now, it's not
because of you but because of Nina, the Portuguese cleaning
woman who sometimes stayed with me for a while in the
evening and really did listen to me, who got all worked up
about my family before I dared to and made it possible for me
to get angry in the first place. Thanks to Nina, who began,
after I confided in her, to realize what was going on, to feel the
coldness and loneliness I grew up in, without any kind of relationships whatsoever. Where is my trust supposed to come
from? Talking to Nina whetted my appetite, I started to eat,
and I realized that life might have something to offer after
all—genuine communication, something I've longed for all my
life. I was forced to take what they called nourishment, but I
didn't want it because it wasn't nourishment at all, it was just
my mother's coldness, stupidity, and fear. My anorexia was a

flight from this spurious, poisoned nourishment. It saved my life; it preserved my desire for warmth, understanding, communication, and exchange. Nina isn't the only one. I know it's there; I know now that what I'm looking for really exists, but all the time I wasn't allowed to know it.

Before my contact with Nina, I didn't know that there were other people besides you lot, my family, and school. Everyone was so normal, so inaccessible. No one understood me. I was "funny." For Nina I wasn't funny. She's a cleaning woman here in Germany; in Portugal she was a student. But she had no money to continue with her studies because her father died just after she graduated from high school, so she had to go out to work. She understood me. Not because she'd been to university, that wasn't the point at all. In her childhood she had a cousin she told me a lot about, and that cousin listened to her and took her seriously. Now she can do the same for me, without effort, without problems. I'm not a stranger to her, though she grew up in Portugal, and I grew up in Germany. Isn't that strange? Here, in my own country I feel like a foreigner, sometimes more like a pariah, just because I don't want to be the way you want me to be.

My anorexia was a demonstration of that. Look at me, see how I look! You find me repulsive? So much the better! That way you'll be forced to realize that there's either something wrong with me or something wrong with you. You look away; you think I'm crazy. Okay, that hurts. But it's still better than being one of you. If I'm crazy, it's because I've moved away from you, because I refuse to adjust, to betray my own nature. I want to know who I am, why I was born, why right now, why here in Germany, why as the child of my parents, who understand nothing about me. Why am I alive? What am I doing here?

I'm glad that since those exchanges with Nina I don't have to hide all these questions behind my anorexia. I want to look for a way of finding answers to my questions and of living in peace with my own self.

November 3, 1997

They've discharged me from hospital because I've regained the minimum weight level. That was good enough, it seems. No one knew why it happened except Nina and myself. Those people are convinced that their diet plan did the trick, that it brought about my so-called improvement. Let them believe it and be happy. I'm just glad to have got out of that hospital. But what now? I have to look for somewhere to live, I'm certainly not staying at home. Mom is as concerned as ever. She invests all her vitality in her concern for me, but her concern gets on my nerves. I'm just afraid that if she goes on like this it'll stop me eating again, because the way she talks to me just kills my appetite. I feel her fear, I want to help her, I want to eat so that she needn't be afraid that I'll start losing weight again. But I can't go on with all that much longer. I don't want to eat so that my mother needn't be afraid I might lose weight. I want to eat because I enjoy eating. The way she treats me takes away all that enjoyment. There are other things she has spoiled for me just as systematically. If I plan to meet Cindy, she says that she hangs around with druggies and is influenced by them. If I phone Klaus, she says all he thinks of is girls, and she doesn't know what to make of him. When I talk to Auntie Isabelle, I can see she's jealous of her sister because I'm much more outgoing with her. I have the feeling that I have to modify and regulate my life so that my mother doesn't flip her lid, so that she's just fine, even if there's nothing left of me. What would that be except anorexia in a psychological sense? Slim yourself down inwardly until there's nothing left that might upset your mother or make her scared.

January 20, 1998

I've rented a room with absolute strangers. I was astonished that my parents let me do it. There was some resistance, but Aunt Isabelle helped me, and in the end I got my way. At first I was very glad to be left in peace without my mother checking up on me all the time. I could organize my day the way it suited me. I was really happy. But it didn't last. Suddenly I was so lonely I couldn't stand it. The indifference of my landlady seemed worse than the constant bossing and interfering by my mother. I had longed for freedom, but now I had it, it frightened me. My landlady, Mrs. Kort, couldn't care less whether I eat or not, what I eat, or when I eat it. I could hardly stand the fact that she didn't care. I started criticizing myself. You don't know what you want, I told myself. If people take an interest in your eating behavior, it gets on your nerves. If they don't care, you can't stand that either. It's hard to meet you halfway. You don't know what you want.

After I'd been talking to myself like this for half an hour, I suddenly heard my parents' voices ringing in my ears. Were they right after all? Did I really not know what I wanted? Here in this empty room, there is no one to stop me from saying what I really want to say. No one interrupts me, no one confuses me, and no one criticizes me. So I decided to find out what I really felt and what I really needed. But at first I found no words to say it. My throat gagged, I felt my tears rising, and all I could do was cry. After I had cried for a while, the answer came all on its own: All I want is for you to listen to me, take me seriously, stop telling me what to do, criticizing me, rejecting me. I want to feel as free with you as I did with Nina. She never told me I didn't know what I wanted. When she was with me, I did know. The way you tell me what to do intimidates me, blocks my knowledge. Then I don't know what to say, I don't know how I have to be so that you're satisfied with me, so that you can love me. But if I did know, would it be love that I'd be getting?

February 14, 1998

When I watch TV and see parents jumping around for joy because their children have won some championship or a gold medal at the Olympics, I get this shivery feeling and ask myself whom they've been loving these last twenty years. The boy who put all his efforts into training and practicing for this moment, for the experience of seeing that his parents are proud of him? Does he feel loved by them? Would they have had this crazy ambition if they had really loved him? Would he have needed to win a gold medal if he had been sure that his parents loved him? Who do they love, in fact? The winner of the gold medal or their child, who maybe suffered from the absence of love? I saw a winner like that on TV. At the moment he heard that he had won, he broke out in tears, bitter tears that shook him through and through. They weren't tears of joy; you could feel the suffering that racked him, though he probably wasn't conscious of the fact.

March 5, 1998

I don't want to be the way you want me to be. And I don't have the courage to be the way I want to be, because I still suffer from your rejection and the loneliness I feel among you. But aren't I lonely because I try to please you? By doing that, I'm betraying myself. When Mom was ill two weeks ago and needed my help, I was almost glad to have an excuse to come back home. But soon I couldn't stand the way she was concerned about me. I can't help it; I always feel that it's insincere in some way. She says she's concerned about me—that's how she makes herself indispensable for me. I experience it as a kind of seduction, seducing me into believing that she loves me. If she really loved me, wouldn't I feel that love? I'm not warped or perverted, I can feel when someone likes me, when someone lets me speak my mind, takes an interest in what I have to say. With Mom all I feel is that she wants me to take care of her and love her. At the same time, she wants me to believe that the opposite is the case. That's blackmail! Maybe I sensed it when I was little, but I couldn't say so, I didn't know how. I only realize that now.

On the other hand, I do feel sorry for her, because I sense her hunger for human relationships, though she is much less aware of the fact than I am, and she's even worse at showing it. It's like she was boxed in somewhere, and being boxed in like that must make her feel so helpless that she has to keep on asserting her power, especially her power over me.

Well, here I am trying to understand her again. Will I never be free of it? I go looking for her, I try to understand her, I want to help her. But it's all pointless. She doesn't want to be helped, she won't relent, and all she seems to need is power. And I'm not going to get drawn into that game anymore. I only hope I can see it through.

Daddy is different. He rules by his absence, he evades everything, makes any kind of encounter impossible. When I was little and he played with my body, he never said anything, not even then. But Mom is different. She is always present, either hollering and criticizing, or displaying her distress and disappointment, complaining about it. I can never withdraw from her presence, but her presence is not nourishing, it's not something I need. It destroys me. Daddy's absence was just as destructive for me, because as a child I desperately needed nourishment. And where can I get it from if my parents refuse it me? The nourishment I needed so badly was the nourishment provided by a genuine relationship, but neither of my parents knew what that was, and they feared a genuine attachment to me because they themselves were abused as children. Well, here I am, back at my old preoccupation, trying to understand my father this time. I did that continually for sixteen years, and now I want to kick the habit. However lonely my father may have been, the fact is that he left me to grow up in that loneliness; he only fetched me when he needed me, but he was never there when I needed him. And later he always kept out of my way. Those are the facts, and I'm going to stick to them. I won't evade reality any longer.

April 9, 1998

I've lost weight again, seriously. The psychiatrist at the hospital gave me the address of a therapist. Her name is Susan. I've talked to her twice. So far, things have gone well. She's different from the psychiatrist. I feel she understands me, and that helps things a lot. She doesn't try to persuade me of anything; she listens, says things herself, says what she thinks, gives me the courage to express my thoughts and trust my feelings. I told her about Nina and cried a lot. I still don't feel like eating, but now I have a clearer and deeper understanding of why that is. They gave me the wrong nourishment for sixteen years, and I've had enough of it. Either I'm going to get myself the right nourishment and find the courage to do so with Susan's help, or I'm going to carry on with my hunger strike.

Is it a hunger strike? I can't see it like that. I just don't feel like eating, I have no appetite; I just don't like food anymore.

I don't like the lies, I don't like the deception, and I don't like the evasion. I'd really like to be able to talk to my parents, tell them about myself, hear them tell me what they experienced when they were small, how they see the world today. They've never talked about that. They always tried to teach me good manners and avoided everything personal. Now I'm sick to death of all that. So why don't I just go away somewhere? Why do I keep coming back home and suffering from the way they treat me? Because I'm sorry for them? True. But I must admit that I still need them, I still miss them, though I know they can never give me what I want them to give me. My mind knows that, but the child in me cannot understand it, has no way of knowing it. It doesn't want to know. All it wants is to be loved, and it cannot understand why it was never given any love, right from the beginning. Will I ever be able to accept that?

Susan says she thinks I can learn to accept that. Luckily she doesn't say that I misinterpret my own feelings. She encourages me to take my perceptions seriously and to believe in them. That's marvelous—I've never experienced that to such an extent before. Not even with Klaus. When I tell Klaus something, he often says, "You just think that's the way it is," as if he could know better what I feel. But poor Klaus, who thinks he's so important, is just mouthing the things his parents told him: "Your feelings are deceiving you, we know better," etc. His parents probably talk that way out of habit, because that's what people say. Actually, they're quite different from my parents. They listen a lot more, and they're much more inclined to engage with what Klaus tells them, especially his mother. She often asks him questions, and you get the feeling she really wants to understand him. I'd be glad if my mother asked me things like that. But Klaus doesn't like it.

He'd rather be left in peace to find things out on his own, rather than having someone try to help him all the time. That's fine, of course, but that attitude of his puts a distance between us. He won't let me get anywhere near him. I think I'll talk to Susan about that.

July 11, 1998

I'm so glad that I have Susan. Not just because she listens to me and encourages me to say things the way I want to say them, but because I know that she's behind me, come what may, and I don't have to change for her to like me. She likes me the way I am. It's overwhelming; I don't have to make an effort to make myself understood. She understands me. It's a marvelous feeling to be understood. I don't have to travel round the world to find people who can understand me and still be disappointed all the time. I have found one person who can do that, and thanks to that person I can gauge how I have always deceived myself, for example with Klaus. We went to see a movie last night, and I tried to talk to him about it afterward. I explained why I had been disappointed, though the reviews were good. He just said, "Your standards are too high." It struck me then that he had made remarks like that before, instead of actually engaging with the content of what I had said. I thought it was normal, because it always happened at home, so I got used to it.

But yesterday it struck me. I thought to myself, "Susan would never react like that—she always responds to what I say, and if she doesn't understand she asks me to explain." Suddenly I realized that I've been friendly with Klaus for a year, but I never dared be aware of the fact that he doesn't listen to me, that he evades me just like Daddy does and that I've been thinking that's normal. Will that change? Why should it?

If Klaus is evasive, he'll have his reasons, and there's nothing I can do about it. I'm just glad I've become aware of the fact that I don't like being evaded. And I've started saying so. I'm not Daddy's little girl anymore.

July 18, 1998

I told Susan that Klaus sometimes gets on my nerves and I don't know why. I like him, after all. It's the little things that annoy me, and I blame myself for that. He's always been good to me. He says he loves me, and I know that I mean a lot to him. So why am I so petty? Why do those little things get me so worked up? Why can't I be more generous? I went on in this way for some time. Susan listened to it all, and at the end she asked what these little things were. She wanted all the details, and at first I was reluctant to answer. But finally I realized that I could go on like this for hours, blaming myself without taking a closer look. And that would have annoyed me, because that way I was condemning my feelings before I could take them seriously and understand them.

So I started telling Susan about the little things. First, there was the business about the letter. I had written Klaus a long letter trying to tell him how much it hurt when he dissuaded me from listening to my own feelings. For example, he would say that I had a negative attitude, or I was splitting hairs, or I was speculating about things that weren't worth thinking about. I shouldn't worry unnecessarily, there was no reason. When he says things like that it gets me down, I feel lonely, and I start telling myself the same things: "Stop brooding, look on the bright side, don't be so complicated." But thanks to the therapy with Susan, I have found out that advice like that doesn't do me any good. It gets me involved in a futile kind of effort, and no good comes of it. I feel the way I am—rejected.

More and more. Rejected by myself, just as much as I was by Mom. How can you love a child if you wish her to be so completely different from the way she is? If I always want myself to be different from the way I am, and if Klaus wants that as well, then I cannot love myself, and I can't believe that others can love me. Who do they love, after all? The person I am not? The person they can change so that they can love me? I won't even try to achieve such "love." I'm tired of it.

Encouraged by my therapy, I wrote all this to Klaus. As I was writing, I found myself fearing at first that he wouldn't understand it. Or else (and that was what worried me most) that he would think I was criticizing him. But I wasn't. I was just trying to be frank and sincere, and I hoped that Klaus would understand me better when he had read it. I made it very clear why I was trying to change myself and that I wanted to include him in the process, not leave him out.

His reply did not come immediately. I was afraid that he'd be angry, impatient with my brooding, I feared his rejection. But I expected him at least to respond in some way to what I had written. After a few days, he wrote me from the place he had gone for a vacation. It was amazing. He thanked me for writing, but he said nothing at all about the things in the letter. He told me what he was doing, the climbing tours he was planning, and the people he went out with in the evenings. I stared at the letter, completely devastated. Of course, I could have shrugged it off, telling myself that my letter had been too much for him. He wasn't used to engaging with other people's feelings, not even with his own, and so he hadn't been able to make head or tail of what I was trying to tell him. But if I was going to take my feelings seriously, this common-sense attitude was no help at all. I felt completely annihilated. It was as if I hadn't written that letter at all. "Who does he think I am,"

I asked myself. "How can he treat me like this?" I felt as if he had dealt me a mortal blow, psychologically.

When I went through those feelings with Susan, I wept like a little child who is genuinely in danger of being killed. Luckily Susan did not attempt to talk me out of my feelings, to tell me that I wasn't in any real danger. She let me cry, took me in her arms like a little child, stroked my back. It was then I realized for the first time that throughout my childhood I had never experienced anything but mortal blows to my inner self. This experience of Klaus simply ignoring my letter was not a new experience. It was an experience I had been all too familiar with. For a very long time. What was new was the fact that I was able to respond to it with pain, pain I could eventually feel. In my childhood there was no one who could have helped me to do that. No one took me in his or her arms; no one had shown me as much understanding as Susan. Pain was something that was inaccessible. Later it manifested itself in my anorexia, but I had not realized that.

Anorexia was telling me something. It was saying I would starve if no one wants to communicate with me. The more I starve, the more the people around me show a total lack of understanding. Just like Klaus's response to my letter. The doctors laid down a series of rules, my parents gave me a whole lot more of them, my psychiatrist threatened me, telling me I was going to die if I didn't start eating and gave me medicine to make me eat. They all tried to force me to work up an appetite, but I had no appetite for the kind of non-communication they were offering me. What I was looking for seemed to be impossible to get.

Up to the moment when I felt that Susan understood me so profoundly. That moment gave me the hope we perhaps all have at birth, the hope that there is such a thing as genuine exchange. Every child tries to make contact with its mother. If there is absolutely no response, it starts losing hope. The root of that hopelessness may well be in the mother's refusal. Now, thanks to Susan, that hope revived. I no longer want the companionship of people like Klaus, who have given up all hope of sharing, the way I once did. I want to meet other people, people I can talk to about my childhood. Most people will probably get scared when I do so. But hopefully there are others who will respond with the same frankness. Alone with Susan, I feel like I'm in another world. I cannot understand how I was able to stick it out with Klaus for so long. The nearer I get to the memory of my father's inhibited behavior, the more clearly I recognize the source of my attachment to Klaus and other friends like him.

December 31, 2000

Today, two years later, I have started rereading the diary I kept during my therapy. This interval is not very long compared with the years of therapy I underwent for my anorexia. Though I was cut off from my feelings, I still hoped, against all the odds, that I might be able to establish a genuine relationship with my parents at some point.

All that has changed now. Therapy with Susan has been over for a year. I no longer need her, because now I can give the child within me the understanding that she gave me for almost the first time in my life. At last I have started being a companion to the child I once was, the child who still lives on inside me. I can respect the signals my body sends me—I have stopped imposing constraints on it. And lo and behold, the symptoms have disappeared! I no longer suffer from anorexia; I have an appetite for food and for life. I have a few friends I can talk to openly without fearing that they will condemn me.

The expectations I once had in connection with my parents have disappeared into thin air, ever since the child in me (and not just the adult part of myself) has understood how totally her longing for contact and communication had been rejected and turned down. I no longer feel attracted by people who can only frustrate my need for openness and honesty. I have found people with the same needs as I have. I no longer suffer from nocturnal palpitations, I no longer feel as if I am traveling down a long, dark tunnel. My weight is normal, my bodily functions are stable, I take no medication, and I avoid contacts that I know would spark off an allergic reaction in me. And I know why that is the case. Among those contacts are my parents and various other relatives who for years gave me "good" advice.

Despite this positive development, the real person behind the figure I call Anita had a massive relapse when her mother managed to coerce her into visiting her again. She had fallen ill and blamed her daughter for her illness: Anita must have known what a blow her withdrawal would be for her mother. How could she do this to her?

This kind of enactment is not surprising. A mother's position frequently gives her unlimited power over the conscience of her adult daughter. The things she was never able to obtain from her own mother as a child—presence and care—are relatively easy to obtain from her grown-up daughter, as long as she can instill guilt feelings in her.

The success of the therapy appeared to be in danger when Anita found herself overwhelmed once again by her old guilt feelings. Luckily the symptoms of anorexia did not reassert themselves. But her visits to her mother made Anita realize that she must reckon with new bouts of depression if she could not summon up the "hardness" imposed on her by this emotional blackmail and break off her visits. Accordingly, she turned once again to Susan, in the hope of support and assistance.

To her amazement, she encountered a Susan she had never known before. Susan tried to explain that she would have to embark on a new stretch of analytic work if she wanted to rid herself completely of her guilt feelings. The work she referred to was the dissolution of her oedipal complex. Susan thought the sexual exploitation by her father had left Anita with guilt feelings toward her mother and thus deepened her dependency on her.

Anita was unable to relate to these interpretations; she felt nothing except anger at being manipulated. She experienced Susan as a prisoner of the psychoanalytic school of thought, a prisoner who, despite all her protestations, had never seriously questioned the validity of those dogmas. Susan had been able to help Anita shake off the patterns of poisonous pedagogy. But now she displayed her own dependence on the views instilled into her by her training, views that sounded completely false to Anita. She was almost thirty years younger than Susan and had no need to submit to dogmas that appeared self-evident to the older generation.

So she took her leave of Susan and sought a group of people of the same age who had been through similar experiences in therapy and had gone in search of forms of communication that had nothing to do with "correction." Here she was given the confirmation she needed to free herself of the pull exerted on her by her family and to prevent her from being talked into theories to which she could not relate. Her depression disappeared, and the anorexia never came back.

Anorexia is generally held to be a very complex condition. The outcome can be fatal. A young woman torments herself to death. She repeats, I would say, what her parents did to her when she was a small child. Unconsciously, she reproduces the sufferings she went through as a child and the way she was tormented to death by parents who refused her the all-important emotional nourishment. This statement appears to be so alarming for many that they prefer to stick to the notion that anorexia is incomprehensible, that it is something that can perhaps be alleviated by medication but never properly cured. The story told by the body is ignored, sacrificed to conventional morality in the name of the Fourth Commandment.

First with Nina, then with Susan, and finally in the group, Anita learned that she had the right to insist on her need for *nourishing communication*, that there was no reason she should be deprived of this nourishment, and that she could not live in her mother's company without paying for it with depression. This insight was sufficient to satisfy her body, which from now on had no reason to remind her of its needs. She had started to respect them, and as long as she was true to her feelings, she was impervious to all accusations of selfishness.

Nina's kindness was Anita's first experience of human warmth and sympathy, free of emotional demands and blame. Then, in Susan, she was fortunate enough to find a therapist who was capable of listening and feeling with her. She identified her own emotions, experienced them, and found the courage to express them. From then on, she knew what kind of nourishment she needed, and she was able to establish new relationships and terminate those from which she expected something without knowing what it was. Now she did know. Susan had given it to her.

Thanks to this experience, she was later able to identify her therapist's own limitations. Never again would she have to look for a hole to crawl into as a refuge from the lies offered to her. From now on, she had her own truth to pit against them. She would no longer have to starve herself. Life was worth living again.

Anita's story requires no further comment. The events she describes provide us as readers with the insight one needs to understand what truly caused her condition. The source of her illness was the hunger caused by deprivation of genuine affective contact with her parents and boyfriend. Her recovery was assured once she realized that today there are people who are willing and able to understand.

CHIEF AMONG THE emotions suppressed (or repressed or disassociated) in our childhood but stored in the cells of our bodies is fear. A child who has been beaten must constantly fear new blows, but it cannot live with the knowledge that it has been cruelly treated. Similarly, a neglected child cannot consciously experience its own pain, let alone express it, for fear of being abandoned entirely. So the child remains trapped in an unreal, rose-tinted, illusory world. That world helps it to survive.

In adulthood, these suppressed emotions are sometimes triggered by quite ordinary events. But the adult cannot relate to them: "Me? Afraid of my mother? Why? She's absolutely harmless; she's nice to me and does her best. How can I be afraid of her?" Or, in another case: "My mother is awful. But I'm aware of the fact, so I've broken off all relations with her, and I'm completely independent of her." This may be true of the adult individual. However, it may also be true that there is still a small, unintegrated child living within, whose panic and fear have never been admitted, never consciously experienced, and thus direct themselves at others. These fears can suddenly assail us without apparent reason and cause us to panic. Unconscious fear of one's father or mother can last for decades if it has not been consciously experienced in the company of an enlightened witness.

In Anita's case, this fear manifested itself in her mistrust of the hospital staff and in her inability to eat. Such mistrust may have been justified, but not necessarily. This is the confusing thing. Anita's body kept on saying: I don't want it. But it could not say what it *did* want. Only after Anita had been able to consciously experience her emotions in Susan's company, only after she had discovered the childhood fears of her emotionally inhibited mother, could she free herself of them. From then on she was better able to come to terms with the present, because she had learned to recognize the difference.

She now knew that it was futile to attempt to force Klaus into a sincere, open-minded dialogue, because it was entirely up to him to change his attitude. Klaus stopped being a substitute mother for her. On the other hand, she suddenly discovered people in her environment who were different from her father and mother, people she no longer needed to protect herself from. As she was now familiar with the story of little Anita, she no longer had to reenact it over and over again. She was increasingly adept at finding her way around in the present and distinguishing *now* from *then*. Her newly discovered pleasure in food reflected the pleasure she took in making contact with people who were receptive to her without her having to make superhuman efforts. She relished her exchanges with them and sometimes wondered what had become of all the mistrust and fear that had separated her for so long from almost all her fellows. In fact, they had disappeared once the present had ceased to be so confusingly entangled with the past.

We know that many young people take a suspicious view of psychiatry. They are not easily convinced that psychiatrists have the best of intentions, even though this may indeed be the case. They expect all kinds of trickery, the arguments trotted out by poisonous pedagogy in favor of conventional morality, everything they have known and suspected since their early years. The therapist has to earn the trust of the patient. But how is this to be done if the patients have repeatedly had their trust abused? Does this mean that the therapist has to spend months, if not years, building up a sustaining relationship?

I do not think so. My experience is that even highly suspicious people will respond if they feel genuinely understood and accepted for what they are. This was Anita's reaction when she met Nina, the Portuguese girl, and Susan, the therapist. Her body quickly helped her to give up her suspicion by developing an appetite for food when it recognized the true nourishment it had been deprived of. The sincere offer of wanting to understand is very easy to recognize because it resists all pretense. If the person making that offer is genuine, not someone who operates from behind a façade, this will quickly be recognized, even by a suspicious youngster. But there must be no trace of deception in this offer of help.

The body would become aware of this sooner or later, and no amount of fine-sounding words would be able to deceive it for long.

Postscript

BEATING LITTLE CHILDREN is a form of abuse that invariably has severe, sometimes lifelong consequences. Violence done to a child is stored in the body and later directed by the adult at other people or even whole nations. Alternatively, the abused child will turn that violence on itself, leading invariably to depression, drug addiction, severe illnesses, suicide, or early death. The first part of this book illustrates how the denial of the truth, the denial of cruelty undergone in childhood, can crucially interfere with the body's biological task of preserving life, and how such denial can block its vital functions.

The idea that we must honor our parents all our lives rests on two pillars. The first consists in the (destructive) attachment of the abused child to his/her tormentors, as manifested not infrequently in masochistic behavior that can take the form of severe perversion. The second pillar is traditional morality, which has threatened us for thousands of years with premature death if we should dare to deny our parents the honor they deserve, regardless of what they may have done to us.

It is not difficult to understand the dreadful effect this morality of intimidation will have on individuals who were abused when they were small. Everyone who has been beaten as a child is susceptible to fear; everyone who was deprived of love as a child will long for it, sometimes their whole lives. This longing contains a whole bundle of expectations, and those expectations, coupled with the fear we have referred to, form an excellent medium in which the Fourth Commandment can thrive. It represents the power of adults over children, and it's reflected unmistakably in all the religions of the world.

In this book I express the hope that, as psychological knowledge grows, the power of the Fourth Commandment will wane in favor of the appropriate respect for the vital biological needs of the body, including truth, loyalty to oneself and to one's perceptions, feelings, and insights. If I seek genuine expression of my feelings in a genuine form of communication, everything that was built on lies and insincerity will fall away from me. Then I will no longer strive for a relationship in which I pretend to have feelings that I do not have, or suppress others that I do have. Love that excludes honesty does not deserve the name of love.

The following points may serve to sum up these ideas:

1. The "love" of formerly abused children for their parents is not love. It is an *attachment* fraught with expectations, illusions, and denials, and it exacts a high price from all those involved in it.

2. The *price* of this attachment is paid primarily by the next generation of children, who grow up in a spirit of mendacity because their parents automatically inflict on them the things they believe "did them good." Young parents themselves also frequently pay for their denial with serious damage to their health because their "gratitude" stands in contradiction to the knowledge stored in their bodies.

3. The *frequent failure of therapy* can be explained by the fact that most therapists are themselves caught up in the snare of traditional morality and attempt to drag their clients into the same kind of captivity because it is all they know. As soon as clients start to feel and become capable of roundly condemning the deeds, say, of an incestuous father, therapists will probably be assailed by fear of punishment at the hands of their own parents if they should dare to look their own truth in the face and express it for what it is. How else can we explain the fact that forgiveness is declared to be an instrument of healing? Therapists frequently propose this to reassure themselves, just as the parents did. But because it sounds very similar to the messages communicated to them in childhood by their parents, albeit expressed in a more friendly way, some patients may need some time to see through the pedagogic angle of it. And even once they finally have recognized it, they can hardly leave their therapist, especially if a new toxic attachment has already formed, if for them, the therapist has become like a mother who has helped them to a new birth (because in this new relationship they have started to feel). So they may continue to expect salvation from the therapist instead of listening to their body and accepting the aid its signals represent.

4. Once clients, accompanied by an enlightened witness, have lived through and understood their fear of their parents (or parental figures), they can gradually start to *break off destructive attachments*. The positive reaction of the body will not be long in coming: its communications will become more and more comprehensible; it will cease to express itself in mysterious symptoms. Then clients will realize that their therapists have deceived them (frequently involuntarily) because forgiveness actually *prevents* the formation of scar tissue over the old wounds, not to speak of complete recovery. And it can never dispel the compulsion to repeat the same pattern over and over again. This is something we can all find out from our own experience.

In *The Body Never Lies*, I have tried to show that some widely held views have long since been exploded by scientific research. Among them are the convictions that forgiveness has a salutary effect, that a commandment can produce genuine love, and that feigning feelings that we do not have is compatible with the demand for honesty. But my criticism of such misleading ideas is by no means to be equated with a refusal to recognize any moral standards or with a wholesale rejection of morality.

On the contrary. Precisely because I staunchly uphold certain values—such as integrity, awareness, responsibility, or loyalty to oneself—I have difficulty with the denial of truths that I consider self-evident and have in fact been empirically substantiated.

Inability to face up to the sufferings undergone in childhood can be observed both in the form of religious obedience and in cynicism, irony, and other forms of self-alienation frequently masquerading as philosophy or literature. But ultimately the body will rebel. Even if it can be temporarily pacified with the help of drugs, nicotine, or medicine, it usually has the last word, because it is quicker to see through self-deception than the mind, particularly if the mind has been trained to function as an alienated self. We may ignore or deride the messages of the body, but its rebellion demands to be heeded because its language is the authentic expression of our true selves and of the strength of our vitality.

Afterword

The Body Never Lies: A Challenge

LMOST ALL MY BOOKS have aroused conflicting
responses. But the emotional intensity with which the
statements I make in my latest book have been affirmed
or rejected is remarkable indeed. The impression I have is that
this intensity of feeling is an indirect expression of the extent to
which the readers in question are close to, or remote from, their
own selves.

After the publication of the original German version of *The
Body Never Lies* in March 2004, many readers wrote to me
saying how relieved they were that they no longer had to feign
feelings they did not really have, or to deny feelings that kept
reasserting themselves. But in other responses, notably in the
press, I have found indications of a fundamental misunderstand-
ing that I myself may have contributed to by using the word "mistreatment" in a much broader sense than is usually the case.

The image this word typically conjures up in our minds is that of a child whose whole body displays the tokens of the physical injuries to which he or she has been subjected. But what I call "mistreatment" in my latest book has much more to do with violations of the child's mental or psychical integrity. Initially those violations remain *invisible*. The consequences frequently appear decades later, and even then it is rare for the connections with the injuries suffered in childhood to be recognized and taken seriously. Both the victims themselves and society in general (physicians, lawyers, teachers, and unfortunately many therapists) prefer to close their eyes to the fact that the real causes of later "disorders" or "misguided behavior" are very often to be found in childhood.

My decision to call these invisible injuries "mistreatment" sometimes arouses resistance and indignant protest. I find this attitude easy to understand because it is one that I shared for a very long time. Earlier, if someone had suggested that I had been cruelly treated as a child, I would have roundly denied the "insinuation." But today I know quite definitely that in my childhood I was exposed to mental cruelty for many years. My dreams, my painting, and not least the messages of my own body have told me this, but as an adult I refused to accept the fact for a long time. Like many other people I thought: "Me? I was never beaten. The few slaps I got were nothing special. And my mother took so much trouble with me." (In my book the reader will find similar statements by others.)

We must not forget that the consequences of early, invisible injuries are so severe precisely because they derive from the trivialization of childhood suffering and the denial of its importance. Adults can easily imagine that they would be horrified and humiliated if they were suddenly attacked by a raging giant many times bigger than themselves. Yet we assume that small children will not react in the same way, although we have all kinds of evidence to indicate how sensitively and competently children respond to their environment (cf. Martin Dornes: *Der kompetente Sääugling*; Jesper Juul: *Your Competent Child*). Parents believe that slaps and spanking do not hurt. Such treatment is designed to impress certain values on their children. And the children end up believing that themselves. Some even learn to laugh the whole thing off and to deride the pain they felt at the humiliations inflicted on them. As adults they adhere to this derision and are proud of their own cynicism, sometimes even making literature out of it, as in the case of James Joyce, Frank McCourt, and many others. If they are assailed by symptoms like anxiety and depression, the unavoidable results of the repression of their genuine feelings, then they will easily find doctors who can give them medication that will help, for a while at least. In this way they can maintain their self-irony, that tried-and-trusted remedy against the feelings asserting themselves from the past. And in so doing they comply with the demands of a society that attaches supreme importance to considerate treatment for parents.

A woman therapist who read my last book thoroughly and understood what it has to say told me that she has now taken a more forthright line in indicating to her clients the injuries inflicted on them by their parents. In almost all cases their response has been to resist the idea. She asked me whether the Fourth Commandment is an adequate explanation of this obstinate attachment to their idealized parents.

My conviction is that, while the Fourth Commandment only

really takes effect with older children, the reasons underlying the clients' almost limitless tolerance of the treatment meted out to them by their parents (so limitless that outsiders sometimes find it hard to credit) goes back to a much earlier stage in their development. Even very small children learn to deny the pain that their parents are so completely unaware of ("a slap doesn't hurt"), to be ashamed of it, to blame themselves for it, or to deride it, as I mentioned above. At a later stage these victims cannot allow themselves to acknowledge that they were in fact victims. Thus in therapy the clients are unable to identify the true culprit. Even if they do experience a resurgence of their suppressed emotions, the truth will have a hard time asserting itself against the mechanisms internalized at such an early stage. After all, those mechanisms have done such long and sterling service in playing down the pain and apparently banishing it altogether. Relinquishing them means swimming against the tide, and that is not only frightening but initially arouses feelings of loneliness. It also exposes us to accusations of self-pity. Yet it is here that the path to genuine maturity, to emotional honesty, begins.

Accordingly, clients aware at the outset of therapy that they were severely injured by their parents and able to take this fact seriously are unusual indeed. People whose parents took their children's feelings seriously from the beginning do not have to make such immense efforts at a later stage to take a serious view of their lives and their sufferings. In the majority of cases, however, the early mechanism remains active: these people obstinately trivialize their own sufferings, even if they are therapists themselves. They remain true to the spirit of Poisonous Pedagogy and to the dictates of the society in which they live. But frequently they are very remote from their own selves. I believe that it is the goal of effective therapy to diminish such self-distance.

Many therapists—though I hope not all—are at pains to divert their clients' attention from their childhood. In this book I show very clearly how and why this happens, though I do not know what percentage of them do this kind of thing. There are, after all, no statistics on the issue. My descriptions will help readers decide whether the therapies they are undergoing are encouraging self-companionship or exacerbating self-alienation. Unfortunately the second of these two alternatives is frequently the case. In one of his books, an author who is highly regarded in analytic circles goes so far as to say that there is no such thing as the "true self" and that it is misleading to talk about it. With therapeutic care based on such an attitude, what chance would adult clients have of identifying their childhood reality? How could they gain awareness of the powerlessness they experienced as children? How could they relive the despair they felt when those injuries were inflicted on them, over and over again, year after year, without being able to perceive their real situation because there was no one there to help them see it? These children had to try to save themselves by taking refuge in confusion and sometimes in self-derision. Adults unable to resolve this confusion at a later stage in a form of therapy that does not impede all access to the feelings will remain prisoners of the derision of their own destinies.

If they do manage to use their present feelings as a key to their simple, justified, and strong emotions as small children and to understand them as comprehensible responses to the (intentional or unintentional) cruelties of their parents or stand-in parents, then they will have nothing more to laugh at. The derision, the cynicism, and the self-irony will disappear—and with them, usually at least, the symptoms that have been the price for this luxury. Then the true self, the authentic feelings and needs of the individual, will become accessible. Looking back on my own life, I am astonished at the single-mindedness, the endurance, and the implacability with which my true self has prevailed against all external and internal resistance. And it continues to prevail, without the help of therapists, because I have become its Enlightened Witness.

Naturally, eschewing cynicism and self-irony is not sufficient in itself to come to terms with the consequences of childhood cruelty. But it is a necessary, indeed an indispensable, precondition for doing so. With an attitude of persistent self-derision we could go through a whole series of therapies without any appreciable progress because we would still be cut off from our genuine feelings and hence from any empathy for the children we once were. What we (or our health insurance) then pay for is a species of therapeutic care that, if anything, helps us to flee from our own reality. And we can hardly expect any change for the better to come about on that basis.

Over one hundred years ago Sigmund Freud subjected himself without reserve to the prevailing idea of morality by putting all the blame on the child and sparing the parents. His successors did precisely the same. In my last three books I have pointed out that while psychoanalysis has become less prone to close itself off from the facts on cruelty to children and sexual abuse and is indeed making an effort to integrate these facts into its theoretical considerations, these attempts are still largely thwarted by the Fourth Commandment. As before, the role of parents in the development of symptomatologies in children is still played down and actively misrepresented. I have no way of knowing whether this so-called broadening of horizons has really changed the attitudes of the majority of therapists. But the impression I get from publications is that reflection on traditional morality has yet to take place. The behavior of parents continues to be defended both in practice and in theory, as was brought home to me by Eli Zaretsky's book *Secrets of the Soul* (2004) with its detailed history of psychoanalysis up to the present (and with no discussion of the Fourth Commandment). This is why my engagement with psychoanalysis is more marginal in *The Body Never Lies*.

Readers unfamiliar with my earlier books may find it difficult to recognize the huge difference between what I have written and the theories of psychoanalysis. After all, analysts focus their attention on childhood to a very large degree and are increasingly open to the idea that early traumas have an impact on later life. But the injuries inflicted by *parents* are still frequently evaded. The traumas usually addressed are loss of the parents, severe illnesses, divorces, natural disasters, wars, and so forth. Here patients feel that they are no longer alone with these traumatic events. Analysts find it easy to empathize with their situation as children, and as Enlightened Witnesses they can provide effective aid in coming to terms with those childhood sufferings, not least because they rarely remind these analytic therapists of their own sufferings. But things are very different when it comes to the injuries that most people have been exposed to, when it comes to perceiving the hatred displayed by one's own parents and later the hostility of adults toward their children.

To my mind, Martin Dornes' interesting and enlightening book (*Der kompetente Sääugling*, 1993/2004) shows clearly how difficult it is to reconcile the notions guiding most analysts with the latest research on infancy, although the author is greatly concerned to convince the reader of the opposite. There are many causes for this, and I have indicated them in my books. But I believe that the main reasons are to be found in the effects of thought blockades (cf. *The Truth Will Set You Free*, 2001, pp. 115–45). Together with the Fourth Commandment, these barriers divert our attention from childhood reality. Freud himself and, above all, Melanie Klein, Otto Kernberg, their successors, and the ego-psychology of Heinz Hartmann have all ascribed to the child what was dictated to them by an upbringing in the spirit of Poisonous Pedagogy: children are evil by nature, or "polymorphically perverse." (In *Banished Knowledge* I have quoted an extensive passage by the highly respected analyst Glover on his view of children.) All this has little to do with childhood reality, and certainly with the reality of an injured and suffering child. As long as corporal punishment and other forms of mental cruelty are almost universally considered to be a legitimate feature of "proper" upbringing, there can be no doubt that the majority of children come under this heading.

Other analysts such as Ferenczi, Bowlby, and Kohut openly addressed this reality. The result was that they have remained on the margins of psychoanalysis because their research was in crass contradiction to the drive theory. Yet as far as I know, none of them left the International Psychoanalytical Association (IPA). Why? Because, like so many others today, they all hoped that psychoanalysis was an open rather than a dogmatic system and that it would be in a position to integrate the findings of modern research. While I do not wish to say that this will never be the case, I do believe that the indispensable prerequisite for such an opening up is the freedom to perceive the real mental injuries incurred in infancy ("cruelty") and to recognize the trivializing attitude of parents to the sufferings of their children. This will only be possible when work on the emotions finds its way into psychoanalytic practice, when there is no longer a fear of the revelatory power of the emotions. Such a development would by no means be necessarily identical with primal therapy. But psychoanalysis must recognize the revelatory power of emotions. Once this happens, the survivors can face up to their early injuries and carve out a path to their origins and true selves with the help of an Enlightened Witness and the messages from their own bodies. As far as I know, this has yet to take place in the framework of psychoanalysis.

In *The Truth Will Set You Free*, I illustrated my criticism of psychoanalysis with reference to a concrete example (pp. 157–65). Here I was able to show that even the creative analyst Winnicott could not really help his colleague Harry Guntrip because he was unable to perceive or deny the hatred that Harry's mother had felt for her son. This example strongly points up the limitations of psychoanalysis that protects the parents, and it was those limits that prompted me to leave the IPA and go my own way. This got me branded as a heretic, what I undoubtedly have been. Unpleasant as it is to be rejected and misunderstood, the situation of a heretic also brought me major benefits. It proved very fruitful for my research, as it gave me the freedom I needed to follow up the issues I really cared about. Suddenly all avenues were mine to explore, and no one could tell me what to think, or dictate what I was allowed to see and what problems I must on no account address. I relish this freedom of thought.

Thanks to this freedom I could afford to take an unsparing view of parents who ruin their children's lives. This meant violating a major taboo. Not only in psychoanalysis but also in society as a whole, such a step is still considered a scandal. "Parents" and "the family" must on no account be presented as a source of violence and suffering. The fear of this knowledge manifests itself quite obviously in most television programs on the subject of violence. (In the recent past I have expressed my views on these issues in various articles on my Web site.)

Statistical surveys on cruelty to children and also the many clients who have reported on their childhood experiences in therapy have led to the establishment of new forms of therapy outside the domain of psychoanalysis. These concentrate on the treatment of trauma and are employed in many hospitals. But even in these forms of therapy (despite the best of intentions about providing empathic care for the patients) the individual's genuine feelings and the true nature of his/her parents can still be disguised, notably with the aid of imaginative and cognitive exercises or spiritual consolation. These so-called therapeutic interventions divert attention from the authentic feelings of clients and the reality of their childhood experiences. Clients require access both to their feelings and to their real experiences if they are to find the way to their own selves and thus dispel their depression. If this is not the case, some symptoms may disappear only to recur in the form of physical ailments as long as childhood reality is ignored. This reality can also be left out of account in body therapy, particularly if the therapist still fears his/her own parents and is thus forced to go on idealizing them.

We now have many reports in which mothers (and, in our childhood forums on the Internet—www.alice-miller.com—also fathers) give honest accounts of how they have been prevented from loving their children as a result of the injuries inflicted on them in their own childhood. We can learn from them, and if we do, we will cease to idealize motherly love at all costs. Then we will no longer be forced to analyze infants as screaming monsters. Instead we will begin to understand their inner worlds, to grasp the loneliness and impotence of children growing up with parents who deny them any kind of loving communication because they themselves have never experienced it. Then we will recognize in the screams of the infant a logical and justified response to the usually unconscious but nonetheless factual and real cruelties of the parents, which have yet to be appreciated as such by society. An equally natural response is the despair of individuals about their damaged lives, a despair that some trauma therapies attempt to alleviate with the aid of "positive thinking." But it is precisely these strong "negative" emotions that enable us to recognize how we must have felt when we were ignored or treated cruelly by our parents. We absolutely need this recognition to eventually overcome the painful effects of the traumas.

Parental cruelty does not always take a physical form (though about 90 percent of the population of the world are beaten in childhood). It can manifest itself above all in the absence of kindness and communication, in oblivion to the needs of the child and its psychic torments, in senseless, perverse punishment, in sexual abuse, in the exploitation of the child's unconditional affection, in emotional blackmail, in the destruction of selfhood, and in countless variations in the exercise of power. The list is endless. The worst thing is that children have to learn to see this as normal behavior because they know nothing else. Children always love their parents unstintingly, whatever the parents do to them.

In one of his books, ethologist Konrad Lorenz gives a sensitive description of the love of one of his geese for a boot. This was the first thing the gosling laid eyes on at birth. An attachment of this kind is instinctive. But if we humans were to follow this natural instinct all our lives (useful as it is at the outset), we would remain well-behaved little children and never enjoy the benefits of adulthood. Among those benefits are awareness, freedom of thought, access to our own feelings, and the ability to compare. The fact that churches and governments have a major interest in impeding this development and leaving individuals in dependency on parent figures is generally well known. What is less well known is the price the body has to pay for it. After all, what would happen if we were to see through the enormities committed by our parents? And what would become of those parent figures if the exercise of their power no longer had any effect?

This is why "parents" as an institution still enjoy total immunity. If that changes one day (as this book postulates), then we will be in a position to feel what our parents' cruelties have done to us. We will have a better understanding of the signals emitted by our bodies and we can live in peace with them, not as the beloved children we never were and can never become, but as open-minded, aware, and perhaps loving adults who no longer have to fear our own biographies because we know all about them.

IN THE RESPONSES to my book I have also come across other misunderstandings, two of which I should like to take up here. They are related to the question of distance over and against cruel parents in cases of severe depression, and to my own personal biography.

First of all I must point out that in the book I repeatedly speak of introjected parents, rarely of real parents, and nowhere of "evil" parents. I give no advice to "Hansel and Gretel," who of course would have to flee their wicked parents. But children can't do this anyway. What I advocate is that we take seriously the genuine feelings that have been suppressed since childhood and that go on eking out an existence in the cellar of the soul. It is understandable that some reviewers who are not familiar with this kind of inner work believe that I am inciting my readers against their "wicked parents." But I hope that readers with slightly more psychological awareness will not overlook the term "introjected."

Naturally I would be glad if the account of my own childhood were to be read with discernment rather than superficially. Ever since I started engaging with the phenomenon of cruelty to children, my critics have accused me of finding it everywhere because I was exposed to it myself. My first reaction to this was astonishment because I knew very little about my early biography at the time. Today I can imagine that the sufferings I fended off may indeed have prompted me to investigate the topic. But what I discovered when I started exploring this subject was not only my own destiny but that of many others. In fact they were my guides and it was thanks to their accounts that I started dismantling my own defenses, looking around, drawing conclusions from the obstinate denial of childhood suffering that have helped me to understand myself. For this I am of course very grateful to those people.

Notes

Introduction: Morality and the Body

1   See Alice Miller, *Breaking Down the Wall of Silence* (New York: Plume, 1997).

2   See Alice Miller, *For Your Own Good*, rev. ed. (New York: Farrar Straus Giroux, 2002).

3   The Adverse Childhood Experiences study is an ongoing project. See, for example, Vincent J. Felitti, "The Relationship of Adverse Childhood Experience to Adult Health: Turning Gold into Lead," available online at www.acestudy.org/docs/GoldintoLead.pdf.

4   See Alice Miller, *The Truth Will Set You Free* (New York: Basic Books, 2001).

2

The Fight for Liberty in the Dramas and the Unheeded Outcry of the Body

1 Friedrich Burschell, *Friedrich Schiller in Selbstzeugnissen und Bilddokumenten* (Hamburg: Rowohlt Taschenbuch, 1958), p. 25; translated by Andrew Jenkins.

2 See Miller, *For Your Own Good.*

3

The Betrayal of Memory

1 Alice Miller, *Thou Shalt Not Be Aware* (New York: Noonday/Farrar Straus Giroux, 1998), pp. 126–27.

2 Louise DeSalvo, *Virginia Woolf: The Impact of Childhood Sexual Abuse on Her Life and Work* (New York: Feminist Press, 1995), p. 132.

3 http://ourworld.compuserve.com/homepages/malcolmi/VWFRAME .HTM. I have corrected Ingram in the first paragraph; he incorrectly identifies Duckworth as Woolf's stepbrother and misstates the age difference between them.

4

Self-Hatred and Unfulfilled Love

1 Yves Bonnefoy, *Rimbaud* (Paris: Seuil, 2004), p. 18.

2 Ibid.

6

Suffocated by Mother's Love

1 Quoted in Claude Mauriac, *Proust* (Paris: Seuil, 1953), p. 10.

2 Marcel Proust, *Jean Santeuil* (Paris: Gallimard, 2001), p. 1051; translated by Andrew Jenkins.

3   Ibid., p. 362.

4   Marcel Proust, *Lettres à sa mère* (Paris: Gallimard, 1953), p. 109; translated by Andrew Jenkins.

5   Ibid., pp. 122–23.

6   Ibid., p. 105.

7
A Past Master at Splitting Off Feelings

1   James Joyce, *Letters of James Joyce*, ed. Stuart Gilbert (London: Faber & Faber, 1966), 1:312.

2   Ibid., 2:48.

9
The Carousel of Feelings

1   See Miller, *Thou Shalt Not Be Aware*, final chapter.

12
Kill Rather Than Feel the Truth

1   Alexandre Garcia, "Patrice Alègre: Portraite d'un Psychopathe," *Le Monde*, June 7, 2003. Available online at www.colba.net/~piermon/ PatriceAlegrePsychopathe.htm

2   See Miller, *For Your Own Good*.

Bibliography

Anonymous. "Lass mich die Nacht überleben." *Der Spiegel*, July 7, 2003.

Becker, Jurek. *Ende des Größenwahns. Aufsätze, Vorträge.* Frankfurt am Main: Suhrkamp, 1996.

Bonnefoy, Yves. *Rimbaud.* Paris: Seuil, 2004.

Burschell, Friedrich. *Friedrich Schiller in Selbstzeugnissen und Bilddokumenten.* Reinbek bei Hamburg: Rowohlt Taschenbuch, 1958.

Chekhov, Anton P. *The Selected Letters of Anton Chekhov.* Translated by Sidonie Lederer. 1955. Reprint, New York: Ecco, 1994.

Damasio, Antonio R. "Auch Schnecken haben Emotionen." *Der Spiegel*, December 1, 2003.

DeSalvo, Louise. *Virginia Woolf: The Impact of Childhood Sexual Abuse on Her Life and Work.* New York: Feminist Press, 1995.

James, Oliver. *They F*** You Up.* London: Bloomsbury, 2002.

Joyce, James. *Letters of James Joyce.* Edited by Stuart Gilbert. London: Faber & Faber, 1966.

Kertész, Imre. *Fateless.* Translated by Christopher C. Wilson and Katharina M. Wilson. Evanston, Ill.: Northwestern University Press, 1992.

Lavrin, Janko. *Dostoevsky*. London: Macmillan, 1947.

Mauriac, Claude. *Proust*. Paris: Seuil, 1953.

Meyer, Kristina. *Das doppelte Geheimnis. Weg einer Heilung—Analyse und Therapie eines sexuellen Missbrauchs*. Freiburg im Breisgau: Herder, 1994.

Miller, Alice. *Breaking Down the Wall of Silence: The Liberating Experience of Facing Painful Truth*. New York: Plume, 1997.

————. *The Drama of the Gifted Child: The Search for the True Self*. Rev. ed. New York: Basic Books, 1996.

————. *For Your Own Good: Hidden Cruelty in Child-rearing and the Roots of Violence*. Rev. ed. New York: Farrar Straus Giroux, 2002.

————. *Paths of Life: Seven Scenarios*. New York: Pantheon, 1998.

————. *Thou Shalt Not Be Aware: Society's Betrayal of the Child*. Rev. ed. New York: Noonday / Farrar Straus Giroux, 1998.

————. *The Truth Will Set You Free: Overcoming Emotional Blindness and Finding Your True Adult Self*. New York: Basic Books, 2001.

Miller, Judith, and Laurie Mylroie. *Saddam Hussein and the Crisis in the Gulf*. New York: Time Books, 1990.

Mishima, Yukio. *Confessions of a Mask*. Translated by Meredith Weatherby. London: Peter Owen, 1998.

Post, Jerrold M. *Leaders and Their Followers in a Dangerous World*. Ithaca, N.Y.: Cornell University Press, 2004.

Proust, Marcel. *Jean Santeuil*. Paris: Gallimard, 2001.

————. *Letters of Marcel Proust*. Translated and edited by Mina Curtiss. New York: Random House, 1949.

————. *Lettres à sa mère*. Paris: Gallimard, 1953.

About the Author

Born in Poland and educated in Switzerland, psychotherapist Alice Miller has written numerous books on the causes and lingering consequences of childhood trauma. She opposes the traditional analytic approach to psychology and declares that the young child's brain can by severely damaged by spanking and other often extremely humiliating child-rearing practices. She has also written a number of pieces on violence and the childhoods of cruel dictators, including *The Drama of the Gifted Child: The Search for the True Self*; *For Your Own Good: Hidden Cruelty in Child-rearing and the Roots of Violence*; and *Thou Shalt Not Be Aware: Society's Betrayal of the Child*. Alice Miller initiated forums on the Internet where survivors of child abuse can share their experiences in different languages (http://www.topica.com/lists/ourchildhood.int) and she also maintains an extensive Web site detailing her work (www.alice-miller.com).

About the Translator

Born in 1949 in South Wales, Andrew Jenkins has translated two of Dr. Miller's previous books. He graduated from the University of Bristol (England) in 1971 and since then has been teaching literary translation, translation theory, philosophy, and practice at the Institute of Translation and Interpreting at the University of Heidelberg (Germany).